Waiting

Waiting

A Nonbeliever's Higher Power

MARYA HORNBACHER

HAZELDEN®

Hazelden
Center City, Minnesota 55012
hazelden.org

Library of Congress Cataloging-in-Publication Data

Hornbacher, Marya, 1974–
    Waiting : a nonbeliever's higher power / Marya Hornbacher.
        p.   cm.
    ISBN 978-1-59285-825-5 (softcover)
    1. Recovering addicts.   2. Twelve-step programs.   3. Agnostics.   I. Title.
    HV4998.H673 2011
    616.86'06—dc22

                                                            2010052243

Editor's note
The names, details, and circumstances may have been changed to protect the privacy of
those mentioned in this publication.
This publication is not intended as a substitute for the advice of health care professionals.
Alcoholics Anonymous, AA, and the Big Book, are registered trademarks of Alcoholics
Anonymous World Services, Inc.

15 14 13 12 11   1 2 3 4 5 6

Cover design by Theresa Jaeger Gedig
Interior design by David Spohn
Typesetting by BookMobile Design and Publishing Services

For Jim A.

This is what you shall do: Love the earth and sun and the animals, despise riches, give alms to every one that asks, stand up for the stupid and crazy, devote your income and labor to others, hate tyrants, . . . have patience and indulgence toward the people, take off your hat to nothing known or unknown or to any man or number of men, go freely with powerful uneducated persons and with the young and with the mothers of families, read these leaves in the open air every season of every year of your life, reexamine all you have been told at school or church or in any book, dismiss whatever insults your own soul, and your very flesh shall be a great poem and have the richest fluency not only in its words but in the silent lines of its lips and face and between the lashes of your eyes and in every motion and joint of your body.

—Walt Whitman, Preface to *Leaves of Grass*

CONTENTS

❦

ACKNOWLEDGMENTS

I would to thank the many people who have helped me find my way toward clarity as I've written this book—those who have questioned, challenged, agreed, disagreed, given me insight and opinion, spoken up, listened well, and given support in so many ways. For a lifetime of conversation, argument, and laughter on the matter of spirituality, thanks especially to my father. For walking her own path and showing me I could walk mine, thanks to my mother. For his wise words one winter evening when The God Issue was making me particularly crazed, thanks to Steve L.—this book would not exist without you. For years of teaching me what spirituality could mean, in all its manifestations, thanks to the Polaris Group, and special thanks to my sponsor. Many thanks to my editor, Sid Farrar, for guiding me so carefully as I wrote. Thanks to family and friends for once again putting up with me during the process. And thanks, above all, to the women I sponsor—for showing me that spirituality lies in action, in connection, and in love.

INTRODUCTION

Using the cycle of a year's passage, we will explore ten spiritual concepts in the context of the seasons of a life and in the practice of the Twelve Steps, looking at how they can be understood by someone who does not believe in a God. Rather than arguments for any theory or philosophy of spirituality, these are explorations of the experience of waiting itself as a spiritual practice.

I walked through the door of the convent. It was a silent Catholic order; no one would speak to me during the time I was going to spend there. I paused in the foyer to listen for something—nuns, God, mice—but there was no sound. The nuns, surely, were somewhere in the building; perhaps God was as well. At least, that was my hope.

The rooms were simple. In the kitchen, I found a long, rough-hewn wooden table with wooden chairs. On the table was a bowl of soup and some bread. This meal was meant for me. I sat down and ate it, after glancing around to see if there might be directions as to what one did prior to eating in a convent—presumably one might pray?—but there were no directions. So I simply ate. When I was done, I washed my bowl and spoon and set them in the rack to dry, and then went to explore the rest of the rooms.

I found a small chapel. The fading light of late day came through the stained-glass windows and cast the pews and stone floor with a bright motley of color. Beyond the chapel, I found a library: the walls were lined floor to ceiling with books, except for one long wall of windows that looked out on an orderly garden, vegetables and flowers in neat boxes and rows. Beyond the garden, there was a labyrinth, the long shadows of trees falling across it.

I scanned the books. I pulled one out, I don't remember which one. I sat down in a chair with the book unopened on my lap. I looked out the window as the light faded and dusk fell.

I had lost, more or less, everything.

I say that in a very qualified sense: I had a place to live, food to eat. I had clothes and the usual things one needs to survive. But I had lost what was most familiar, what was safest, what I knew best: I had lost an addiction. That addiction had been the center of my existence since I was a child. It had been my guiding principle, my closest companion, the thing I turned to for comfort, for answers, for assurance that I would be all right. It had been my god.

It had nearly killed me.

I fought like hell to keep it. I kicked and screamed and swore and sobbed. I begged to be allowed to hold it just a little while longer. But in the end, I had to let it go.

And without it, I was quite lost.

I didn't know why I had come to the convent. It was an impulse; someone had told me there was a convent in a nearby city, an order of nuns who had taken a vow of silence and who allowed guests to stay. In that moment, the idea of going somewhere to be entirely silent appealed to some part of me I couldn't explain. Maybe I thought that if things got quiet enough, I would hear God.

Night fell over the convent. I sat there in the dark, watching the moon scatter light over the orderly garden. There was no sound except that of my own breath.

I set the book on a table, picked up my small bag, and found the stairs up to the room where I was to sleep. In this room, there was a narrow bed, a simple desk, and a prayer bench, the velvet kneeling rail well worn. I set my bag on the floor and studied the prayer bench awhile. Then I lay down on my back on the bed and stared at the ceiling.

I was at the lowest point in my life. I had lost all I thought I needed. I did not know how to go on.

It was an enormous, sudden peace.

I knew, very quietly, that I would not find God in this place. I knew it was possible I would not find God at all. And so I could not explain the overwhelming peace I felt. I could not explain how I knew, absolutely, that it would be all right.

I remembered the words of Julian of Norwich: *And all shall be well, and all shall be well, and all manner of thing shall be well.*

I could not have articulated it at that time, but what I felt that night is what I would now call grace. I felt faith. I heard something. Not the voice of God, not the beating wings of angels. Not the murmur of nuns at prayer, not even the scuttle of mice.

What I heard was the stirring of my own spirit coming to life.

—

The spirit, it seems to me, grows noisy and goes silent by turns over the course of one's life. There are ways in which we silence it. Many of us have silenced it through addiction, but there are other ways, and many of us have used those as well. And there are ways in which we can draw the spirit out, listen for it with all the strength we've got.

But listening for spirit is something of a complicated process when we do not believe in a God, or do not feel a connection to what may be called a Higher Power. Many of us have been trained to think of "spirituality" as the sole provenance of religion; and if we have come to feel that the religious are not the only ones with access to a spiritual life, we may still be casting about for what, precisely, a spiritual life would be without a God, a religion, or a solid set of spiritual beliefs.

Throughout this book, I use the words *spirit* and *spiritual* often, and that may seem strange when I state my own lack of belief in a Higher Power or God. And some days it seems strange to me as well, that I am so certain of an ineffable force within me and within all of us when I doubt the presence of a metaphysical power without. But really, it isn't contradictory. I am not speaking of metaphysics. I am speaking of the thing in ourselves that stirs.

The origin of the word *spirit* is Greek. It means "breath." That which stirs within, slows or quickens, goes deep or dies out. When I speak of spirit, I am not speaking of something related to or given by a force outside ourselves. I am speaking of the force that *is* ourselves. The experience of living in this world, bound by a body, space, and time, woven into the fabric of human history, human connection, and human life. This is the force that feels and thinks and gives us consciousness at all; it is our awareness of presence in the world. It is the deepest, most elemental, most integral part of who we are; it *is* who we are.

So when I speak of spirit, I'm speaking of something that frustratingly defies articulation, because we have few words for spiritual beyond those that refer back to a God. But not believing in a God is not opposed to a belief in an aspect of the *self* that can be called spiritual. The latter is experienced, and defined, very personally, and is different for each individual.

I am not speaking of some universal or transcendent "Spirit" that exists outside of us; I am speaking of the human *spirit* that exists in each of us. I'm speaking of something that is urgently important in ourselves, the very thing that's sent us searching, the thing that feels the longing, the thing that comes knocking on the door of our emotionally and intellectually closed lives and asks to be let in.

When we let it in, and only when we do, we begin to be integrated people. We begin to find integrity in who we are. We are not just a body, not just a mind, not just a mass of emotions, not just people dragging around the dusty bag of our pasts. We have depth and wholeness, not shattered bits of self that never seem to hold together properly. And we begin to walk a spiritual path.

This path is not toward a known entity of any kind. Rather, it is the path that leads *through*. And there are many points along the way where we stop, or we fumble, or we get tangled up or turned around.

And those are the places where we wait. We're not waiting for the voice of God, or for the lightning-bolt spiritual experience. We're not waiting to be saved or carried. We're waiting for our own inner voice—for lack of a better word, I'm going to keep calling it spirit—to tell us where to go next.

It will.

I confess: even after putting together a few sober days, I still flinch at the God-centered language of the Twelve Step literature. There's no need to lay out a litany of examples; one need only thumb through the Big Book (*Alcoholics Anonymous*) or *Twelve Steps and Twelve Traditions* or a meditation manual to find what I'm talking about. And I imagine if you've picked up this book, you're probably already aware of what can seem like an inherent assumption held by the Twelve Step program: sooner or later, you will believe in God.

Let's be clear—not every Twelve Step member feels this way. There are plenty of people who are completely comfortable with the idea that some do and some do not believe in or feel a connection to a Higher Power. But there are also a whole lot of members who don't mind telling you that you need a God and better find one quick, or risk losing your sobriety. They believe what they believe. They just don't believe what I believe.

But the literature itself does seem to press the point—sometimes none too gently—that a relationship with God is a basic necessity for contented, long-term sobriety. Maybe the most striking moment when the newcomer realizes this is in reading "How It Works." It reads: "Remember that we deal with alcohol—cunning, baffling, powerful! Without help it is too much for us. But there is One who has all power—that One is God. May you find Him now!" (pages 58–59).

That's religious language. Not spiritual language. It leaves no room for interpretation. It implies—rather, it *states*—that without the help of the One God (whose, or which, One God is not made clear), you can't get sober.

So while many of us have spent a lot of time telling non-AAs "no, no, it's not a religious program!" I have to concede that it certainly looks like one from time to time.

Generally speaking, when a person expresses doubt about God, or flat-out says he or she doesn't believe in one, people get a little frustrated. It's as hard to explain belief as it is to explain unbelief, but people want to share what has helped them, and many of them want you to be able to find the God that works in their lives. So they direct you to read chapter 4 of the Big Book, "We Agnostics."

We get a few paragraphs in. We think we may actually have found some room for our own beliefs within this program. And then we are instructed, "Cheer up, something like half of us thought we were atheists or agnostics. Our experience shows that you need not be disconcerted" (page 44).

In other words—you are not *really* an atheist or an agnostic. You are deluded. You are simply not as far along in sobriety or spiritual development as those who believe in a Higher Power. Soon enough, you'll believe in one too.

The chapter ends with a description of a man sent to his knees by a thunderbolt of a thought: *"Who are you to say there is no God?"* By this point, after many pages of reading about the apparent *fact* that there is a God, and the absolute necessity of belief in one if we hope to hold on to sobriety, the nonbeliever may be despairing, furious, alienated, or simply at a loss. In any case, we may feel very strongly that there is no room for us in this kind of spiritual context.

But such a spiritual experience is only one kind. There are as many ways of being spiritual, of feeling one's spirit stirring, of creating a spiritual practice in one's life as there are people in the world. The task is to get to know our own spiritual nature, learn what feeds it, and act from a spiritual place in our work in the world.

I was one of those people who came into the Twelve Step program and was more confused by the notion of a Higher Power than opposed to it. I figured there might be one out there, and if all these people were sure there was, they were probably right and could likely tell me how to find it.

Gradually, though, it began to seem that the belief in God—not just a Higher Power, not just a "God of your understanding," but a God who was assumed to be of *all* our understandings, even those of us who had no understanding of, or belief in, a God at all—was a given. I got the sense that if I did not believe in God now, it was a matter of me still being new to sobriety, and surely I'd come to my senses soon.

So I gave it a shot. Every morning I watched the sun rise and read a highly religious little meditation book and tried having a conversation with God. I waited for that sense of the presence of a Higher Power that I'd heard of. I chastised myself for not being open to real spiritual experience. It was one of the loneliest things I've ever done.

It sent me, actually, to a pretty bad place. I was terrified I was going to lose my sobriety. I wanted to know what was wrong with me that I couldn't sense or believe in the existence of a God, let alone the personal involvement in my life one might have. I spoke of it in meetings, this failure on my part; I talked to my sponsor, to other people in the program, to anyone I thought might be able to instruct me how to find this God of which everyone spoke in such personal, intimate terms.

Finally, someone pulled me aside after a meeting. He said, "Here's the thing. I don't know what God is, or if there is a God. I only know that there are moments when I feel spiritual. I can be in a church or a mosque or a temple or a grocery store or the woods. And I get that sense of *being spiritual.* Of something alive in me. It's not necessarily a sense that something outside me is present. It's the sense that *I* am present. Completely present. Alive."

And in that moment, as we stood there in the church basement kitchen while people around us rustled and chattered and headed home, I recognized that what I felt—a connection to this person, an ability to hear him clearly, to open my mind, to listen, and to learn—was a spiritual experience. It was an enormous relief. I stopped feeling like I was doing the whole thing wrong. His words undid the terrible tangle I was in, and I could move forward with a new sense of what spirit meant, and what mine felt like, and what I believed.

For all its God language, the Twelve Step program isn't actually an attempt at religious conversion. Really, it just tries to bring us to a place of new spiritual understanding that allows us to live differently *in this world.* The Steps are not intended to get us to heaven or save us from hell. This is not about life in another world, above or below. This is about how we live *here.* And though many would not agree with me on this point, it's my contention that how we live *here* is defined and guided by who we are, who we choose to be, who we try to become. Some believe that a God is the guiding force and principle in this evolution in ourselves. I believe what guides us is already *in* us, is in fact the deepest part of who we are—capable of turning us into ever-more spiritually grounded, spiritually generous, peaceful people.

That evolution itself is a spiritual process. And the Steps can be guideposts on the way. Each of them asks deep and hard spiritual questions; while some of us may need to find our way past the God-centered language to reach the core of those questions, we can find that core, and having done so, can open our minds to what the Steps might teach us about how to live. The Steps are intended—it sounds simple, and it is—to make us better people, more aware, more alive, and more spiritually whole.

The Steps, at their heart, are a pathway to spiritual experiences. Not to a singular spiritual experience. They are, as you'll often hear in meetings, "a program for living." I would add that they are a program for living *spiritually*. Each Step is based on spiritual principles; taken as a whole, they form a map toward understanding ourselves better as spiritual people. And they are a spiritual *practice*, requiring not only thought and feeling but action as well.

We come to the program "spiritually bankrupt." We come spiritually bereft. Addiction starves and eventually kills the spirit; we come in need of spiritual nourishment. That nourishment comes in different forms for different people. For some it comes as God, for some it's felt as a more amorphous Higher Power. Some people are comfortable taking the suggestion often given to nonbelievers, that they make their Twelve Step group their Higher Power. Some people, for reasons I don't claim to understand, find comfort in the idea that literally anything can be their Higher Power—a doorknob, a rock.

Whatever works. But it is human nature to want some source of spiritual comfort or guidance—the things a God gives to those who believe. Addicts have, over the years of their use, ultimately made their addiction their Higher Power. And when addicts come to sobriety, the sense of disorientation—the sense of being unmoored from anything solid—the sense that they are absolutely lost is overwhelming.

So we reach for something. We reach blindly outward—toward a God in whom we may or may not believe, toward a Higher Power we may not understand, toward a group of people, toward a simple inanimate thing. And for some of us, this works. We find that spiritual source we crave.

Some of us, though, do not.

It is my belief that though we need to reach outward in our search for spiritual nourishment, we need to reach deeper within. For those of us who do not know God, who may not believe there is a God to know, this search within is the search for our own spiritual nature. We seek not what is out there in some abstract heaven. We seek, instead, what is here, in ourselves, on this earth.

And the search can be undertaken using the Steps. Though the language of the old program literature is religious, its message is spiritual, and it seeks to bring about a spiritual experience. And if we allow it to, it does. We do not need to know a God for that to happen.

The practice of the Steps does not require houses of worship or prostrations or adherence to a creed. It requires a careful and intensive look inward, a deepening knowledge of ourselves, our actions, and our beliefs, so that we can be more intimately, spiritually connected to the world in which we live. The Steps ask us to take that look inward, and ultimately bring us to a spiritual wholeness where we have the capacity to love and serve the world outside our limited selves.

When we come to the program, we are in dire need of a spiritual source. The Steps lead us to it, whatever we call it, whatever it may look like, whatever form it may take. This source feeds us; and, in turn, we are able to feed others in spiritual need.

This is a spiritual experience. This is a spiritual experience anyone may have, anyone who knows a God, and anyone who does not. This is a way of living a spiritual life; this is a spiritual practice of being alive.

—

Before we go any further, I assure you that this book will ask more questions than it answers. It will not offer an "alternative" set of beliefs that are hard and fast in any way. It will not posit an alternative God or gods. It will not build a ladder to a clearly knowable Higher Power. Part of me wishes I could find these things for myself.

But another part of me has come to know this: it is precisely in my lack of certainty—about whether there is a God, about what the spirit actually is—that I find my spirituality. I have come to believe that, for me, peace can only be found in the acceptance of all I do not know.

I do not know if there is a God, if there is a Higher Power. In the interest of full disclosure, I do not, myself, believe that there is a personified God, a deity to whom I pray and by whom I am guided and who intervenes in my daily life. I do not find a source of comfort in a singular religious or spiritual figure, nor do I have a God to question when things go wrong in my life or in the world.

That I myself do not have or know such a God does not mean one does not exist. It only means I do not believe it exists. I am only one, incredibly flawed, absolutely limited human mind—one spirit—among millions more. But it is precisely this limitation—the fact that I can know only so much of the nature of things, of spirit, of universal truth—that is, paradoxically, the source of my spirituality.

Because, lacking a sense of a God above, but aware of the spiritual nature of myself—the spiritual nature of, I believe, all human beings—I find myself in need of a spiritual life here on the ground. A spiritual life that is not theoretical, but practical. A way of living spiritually—here, in this life, bounded by space and time, both in connection with others and in solitude, here in this living world.

This book, then, is not an attempt to find or name a God. It is not a search for a spiritual source outside ourselves. It is, instead, a search within—for what we mean when we refer to *spirit*, for what our own spirit feels like, for how we can live according to that spirit's wisdom.

In this book, I want to move beyond "There is no God" (or "Is there a God?") to "What do I believe?" What do we believe about the human, the spirit? And beyond that, I hope we can move from asking ourselves what we believe, to a place where we can ask, "How do I live?"

To me, that's the central question. How do I live in a spiritual way?

How can the Steps be worked in a spiritual way, if we do not believe in a God? That's an oddly easy question to answer: the Steps can't *not* be worked in a spiritual way. They are spiritual steps, leading to spiritual experiences. The only requirement is that we open ourselves to them. If we let them, the Steps will work themselves into us, and we will work them as spiritual people, increasingly aware as we go of our spiritual nature, our spiritual strength.

This book takes the form of a year on a spiritual journey. I am not trying to reach God by December; I am not trying to develop a fixed set of beliefs in twelve months. I am merely going through the Steps, trying to draw out the spiritual principles that shape them, that build on the previous Step and lead to the next.

If I am searching, I am searching for a deeper understanding of spirit, of spirituality, of a way in which one can live a spiritual life. I hope to find, on my way, greater insight into what makes people spiritual beings—in their brokenness, in their wisdom, in their joy, in their despair. And I hope to find a way to articulate what I mean when I speak of the spiritual practice that can be put into action by working the Twelve Steps.

The Steps have shed light on a spiritual self I did not know I possessed. I have heard that same thing from more people than I can count—believers, nonbelievers, atheists, agnostics, none of the above. The Steps are not a religion, not by any means. But they pave the way, for those who need them, to a spiritual source. Taking us from brokenness and isolation, to awakening and connection, to, finally, spiritual awakening and action, we find as we go that the spiritual source can be found within and without, in ourselves, in others, right here in this world.

❦

CHAPTER ONE

Despair

January

Reaching the end of a given road in our lives—or the end of the road of our lives in addiction—we find ourselves at a point of despair, recognizing our powerlessness, not knowing where to go next or if we can even begin again. Sometimes it's a matter of waiting through this painful moment, allowing the heart to experience what comes, to feel its way through darkness, and to emerge with whatever it finds. We have come to Step One.

Lake Superior sprawls endlessly to the east of Highway 61, a steely silver-gray, surging against the rocks that line the shore. Sharp outcroppings of rock rise high above the road. At certain crevices, icy waterfalls tumble downward, frozen solid, as if time had stopped and held the ropes of water tangled in midair.

This is the heart of winter in the deep north. For reasons I can't quite explain, I'm driving yet farther north, toward the Canadian border, toward tundra, a place where maybe the landscape will match the emptiness I feel spreading through my chest.

There are times when the heart burrows deeper, goes tunneling into itself for reasons only the heart itself seems to know. They are times of isolation, of hibernation, sometimes of desolation. There is a barrenness that spreads out over the interior landscape of the self, a barrenness like tundra, with no sign of life in any direction, no sign of anything beneath the frozen crust of ground, no sign that spring ever intends to come again.

I have known these times. I believe everyone has. And for the better part of my life, I have tried to dull the sharp awareness of them with addictive substances and behaviors. I have tried to blot them out, blunt their edges, make them disappear. At those times in my life when I have reached a moment of doubt or despair, I have turned in desperation to my addictions, clinging to the absolute faith that my addictions would fill the emptiness. I have trusted the voice of addiction to guide me; I have made it the absolute in my life, the one thing I trusted and knew to be true. I have tried, again and again, to turn my addictions into a spiritual source.

Addiction failed me, as it fails us all. Its clear voice turned out to be nothing more than the voice of my own fear. The source of guidance and comfort it seemed to be were false at best, deadly at worst. And eventually I realized that my life in active addiction had to end. The devastation it had created in my life, in the lives of those around me, in what I wanted to be myself, was too great.

But at that moment—the moment of realization that life as I'd been living it would have to end—I felt devastation unlike any I'd ever known. The barrenness was indescribable. The emptiness that opened up in me seemed to stretch on forever; I could see no end to it, could find no source of comfort in it, could not imagine any way out.

That state of devastation, of despair—a state we fear and run from, most of us, all our lives—is a spiritual state. It does not feel like it at the time. It feels powerfully, absolutely alone. We have reached an ending; we know that the path we've been on goes no further or leads only deeper into a private hell. It is what they call the dark night of the soul.

But it *is* a spiritual state: because in that darkness, we become aware of a spiritual hunger that we know must be fed. And that awareness of ourselves as spiritual beings is in fact a gift. It is a turning point. We reach an ending, yes, but it is at that ending where we hear our spirits, which we'd thought were long buried or dead, choke back to life.

Although I spent years drowning the sound of my spirit in alcohol, hoping it would serve as some kind of spiritual nourishment, there came a time when I had to stop. And though it was the most terrifying thing I had ever done, I turned inward. I turned to face what seemed to be a spiritual wasteland, walked into it without compass or map, in the hope that I could find my way to something I might need.

At the lip of a cliff, I look out over Lake Superior, through the bare branches of birches and the snow-covered branches of aspens and pines. A hard wind blows snow up out of a cavern and over my face. I know this place, I know its seasons—I have hiked these mountains in the summer and walked these winding pathways in the explosion of color that is a northern fall. And now, as the temperature drops well below zero and the deadly cold lake rages below, I feel the stirrings of faith that here, in this place, in my heart, spring will come again.

But first the winter must be waited out. And that waiting has worth.

—

Most of us, when we arrive at the realization that we have reached a spiritual dead end, come to that knowledge broken, barely holding our pieces together. We come craving wholeness. We come craving comfort. Those of us facing the end of addiction are painfully, terrifyingly aware of our own powerlessness, our tininess in the face of something vast. It has nearly destroyed all we have and are.

And yet we miss it. We feel that we need it. Addiction was the thing that brought us a kind of comfort. We answered to it, and so it seemed to give us guidance. It was what we knew. Without it, we feel hopelessly lost. Lost, grieving, desperate, emptied of the things we knew.

The Big Book calls us spiritually bankrupt. This spiritual bankruptcy is characteristic of both those who have a sense of a Higher Power and those who do not. People who know and feel connected to a God feel just as lost when they decide to stop their addictive behavior. Their grief in loss is no less; they speak of the same disorientation and sense of absence that those of us without God speak of, and their devastation is the same.

All of us, at one time or another in our lives, reach a point where we are absolutely leveled by some loss or by another spiritual crisis. Yet I believe we need to reach it, or we will not fully hear the echo of a spiritual emptiness within; and until we hear that echo, we will not respond.

But now that we have reached that point, what do we do? What should we feel? Where do we turn?

That last may be the most pressing question for those of us who do not believe in God. Here at the nadir of emotional and spiritual experience, we want lifting up out of this dark place. We long for comfort. We desperately need guidance. And who or what, many of us are asking, will give us those things? What lifts us, when we have fallen so far? To what source do we turn?

This state of spiritual brokenness is more than painful. It is terrifying. And the absence of a belief in a Higher Power makes us feel as though there is an enormous silence that comes when we ask these questions. That silence is lonely, and frightening, and it makes the sense of longing, need, and emptiness within us even greater.

But we are not ultimately empty, and there is more to hear than silence. We are not yet listening to our own spiritual voice. We are unaccustomed to doing so. We are also not looking to the people around us for spiritual wisdom. And we have not yet learned to look to the Twelve Step program itself as what it is: A program for living. A program for living *spiritually*. And a path to spiritual experience.

But now we are only embarking on the journey. Our craving for spiritual wholeness is enormous. Our education in who we are as spiritual people is only beginning. It is a lifelong process and will move through many phases. We will come to this point again—this point of darkness, of despair, of loss and loneliness and grief. And so we must pay attention while we are here. We must experience this spiritual stage fully and with consciousness. And we must wait.

When we are faced with the choice between our own certain destruction and the uncertainty of going on, we are told that there is a spiritual solution to our problem, a way of living that will save us from the spiritual death we were already in. But for many of us, "spirit" and "spiritual" are suspect concepts. And we're asking: What is spirit? Can it exist separate from the notion of a God? *Is* there anything within us that can be called spiritual?

So much of our sense of the spiritual has been killed off. Our ability to recognize and experience joy, beauty, or wonder has been destroyed. Our ability to connect with other people in a real and intimate way has been damaged beyond recognition, to the point where many of us do not know what a healthy or fulfilling relationship with another person would be.

Both of those things—the internal sense of awe at the beauty and difficulty of life, and the ability to truly connect with other people—are spiritual experiences, and we have cut ourselves off from them through our addiction.

So when we ask ourselves whether there is anything within us that is spiritual, whether we have, in fact, a *spirit*, we can look back to the time prior to our addiction. For many of us, that was childhood. It is easy to write off childlike faith in the universe and childlike wonder at the world as simply a lack of knowledge about "how life really is." Well, how is life, really? Do we know—we who have been denying life, life's beauty and its true challenges, for such a long time? Or did we know better as children, when the whole world seemed to be filled with meaning and possibility, both good and bad?

We do each have spirit within us. But we have to recognize that it is deeply buried under layer after layer of addictive sickness. That spiritual voice we long to hear has been silenced by our own years of use and abuse. In this first stage of our journey, we begin the long archaeological dig that will lead us to our own spiritual truth.

The spiritual journey moves forward and back, goes around in spirals, descends and ascends again. It is not a straight shot from the depths of despair we feel now to the grace we hope to feel soon. We will feel despair again, and feel grace many times, and feel wonder and doubt, and feel myriad things that we have not felt in a very long time. We will feel these things in our core, at a spiritual level, the level of ourselves that has been ignored for so long. We have been barely living, living only at the surface of what is possible in human experience. Now that we have set out on a path toward a greater sense of a spiritual life, we will feel more, feel deeply, feel both joy and pain. And we will feel our spirits bloom. We will hear that spiritual voice, first softly, then with increasing clarity, until it becomes as natural a part of us as breathing.

This is the spiritual experience we seek: to find our spiritual selves, so that we may connect with the world in a spiritual way.

To make this beginning requires bravery—even the bravery of desperation—and it also requires faith. Faith does not imply a God; the faith we need is a faith that spiritual growth and wholeness are possible for us. It may seem unlikely. But we have journeyed here, from the certainty that nothing could help us to the tentative hope that something can. That took faith. It was a spiritual leap to come even this far. It required us to reach deep within ourselves and come up with whatever tiny sliver of hope we might have left. And we did that. So we hold on to that hope, that tentative faith, as we begin.

There is a place in spiritual life for descent. It is unavoidable in life that there will be loss, there will be grief, there will be moments—or months, or years—when we doubt that there is meaning or purpose to our lives or to human life at all. And at these moments, we descend.

The end of our addictive use is such a moment. We are thrown into doubt, and it may feel as if we are tumbling end over end into a dark and deeply unfamiliar place, a place where we have no guide. Without God, what guides us through and out of this place?

Wait. It isn't always necessary or even desirable to leave this place so soon. There may be things we need to learn from how we feel—the emptiness, the grief, the fear. We need to learn the nature of these things, because the end of our addiction is not the only time in our lives we will feel them. The descent into this dark place can be a moment for spiritual development if we allow it, if we acquaint ourselves with the nature of that darkness, and if we begin to trust ourselves—our spirits—to find the way back to light.

If we think about it, we realize that we know despair well. The end of our addictive use brought us to levels of sickening despair that we could not answer with any hope. And that's the difference: now that we have begun working toward spiritual wholeness, we *can* see that hope is possible for us. We may doubt. We may still be profoundly grieving our loss. But we are no longer trapped in the torturous cycle of turning *to* addiction in an attempt to comfort the despair *of* addiction.

At times, it may seem worse—harder, at least—to live through the despair of this loss without the temporary comfort of our addictive behavior. We cannot drown our sorrows. We must face the fact that we don't know, really, where we are, how we got here, how long the pain will last, or how to move past it. That uncertainty may be the most painful part of not knowing a God: no one is there to reassure us that a God will take the pain and confusion away. We simply don't know. And we have no way to numb ourselves or forget the condition we're in.

But until we do this work—until we plumb the depths of our emotional and spiritual nature—we will never truly know who we are. We have been hiding from ourselves for the duration of our addiction. And until we explore the darker moments of the human experience, we will never be spiritually whole.

And so it's necessary to learn to trust our spirits to keep us safe on this journey. This is an act of faith: we must trust that we will emerge.

We are often told that it is God who will lift us out of the spiritual abyss we're in. It may be true. Even so, it isn't necessarily something all of us can believe. But there are three things in which we can place our faith: our own spiritual integrity and strength, the spiritual nature of those with whom we form connections, and the cycles of spiritual life.

And we can also place our faith in the process of working this particular spiritual program of the Twelve Steps. So, as we begin to work the Steps, we attempt to work each one in a spiritual way. For now, all that requires of us is that we open our minds and hearts to the possibility that the Steps can be what they claim: a path to spiritual experience. We do not need to believe in a God; we do not need to believe that we *will* believe in a God; we only need to begin to conceive of ourselves as spiritual beings who are capable of making a spiritual connection with the world.

So we begin our work by opening our hearts and minds, paying attention, and giving ourselves over to the possibility that we will be spiritually changed.

The notion that we are powerless is powerful, and for many of us painful. We have suffered under the delusion that we were in control of our addiction for a long time, and the realization that we are under *its* control is very hard to accept.

But the word has ramifications beyond our addiction. Spiritually speaking, we are asked here to recognize our smallness in the face of certain forces—in the first case, the force of addiction itself. But we also must recognize our smallness in the face of a universe we do not fully know or understand, which operates on principles of its own, which moves us, rather than us moving it.

Many people believe the source of that universal movement is God; in the Christian tradition, there is the faith that God "moves in mysterious ways," and that faith may bring comfort when one doubts the meaning or purpose of events. For those of us who do not believe in God, though, it may be simply terrifying to recognize that the universe—not a person, not a logical mind—operates according to laws we cannot, and will not, understand.

But those laws, when looked at without fear, are awesome and miraculous in their own way. That we are a part of that awesome greater whole is astonishing as well. To me, an acceptance of my humanness—my unknowing, the fact that I am irrevocably tethered to the ground, that I am not much more than a fleck of matter in an infinite cosmos, but an *integral* fleck—is a spiritual practice. Accepting my humanness, I am put in my place; I am able, in this place, to feel the overwhelming spiritual wonder at the mysteries of this world.

So when we find ourselves wondering about the powerful nature of our addiction and our helplessness before it, we often also wonder about the nature of massive, infinite, universal forces, and our tininess in the face of all that exists beyond ourselves. But this is exactly what we need to face. We *are* tiny; we are powerless. We are, by our very human nature, limited in what we can know or do or control or change.

And this is a moment of grace, this recognition. We are recognizing that there *are* things—forces, powers—that are "greater than ourselves." These forces do not need to wear a face or have a name or creed. They exist according to their own laws and logic, and we do not need to understand them; we need only acknowledge that they are there, and while we are a part of them, we are not the powerful forces they are. This is simply a recognition, and an *acceptance,* of the fact that we are human and there is much beyond us; there is much that is more powerful than we are; there are powers greater than ourselves that we do not need to understand as a God.

And here we discover that in a state of despair, facing that excruciating truth, recognizing our powerlessness—we are beginning to have a spiritual experience.

When we face the moment of spiritual crisis that is addiction's depth, we have to recognize that our lives have become unmanageable. We may struggle with denial about this, as we may struggle with denial that we are powerless, but ultimately we must realize the truth of it. The degree of our unmanageability is irrelevant; what we are looking at from a spiritual point of view is the fact that our *spiritual* lives are most definitely unmanageable. They may be buried, they may be in chaos, but they are not in any state of development, and we are not at peace.

The principle of unmanageability reminds us that a life wherein we are divorced from our own spiritual selves and from the spiritual sources around us—a life where we have replaced true spiritual sources with addiction—is a life without center and will spin out of control. There is nothing to ground that life. There is nothing to ground us ourselves, to give us a sense of wholeness or integrity.

And in this kind of spiritual crisis, we feel nothing if not a lack of integrity. We feel literally *disintegrated.* Our lives are split into parts; we run from the past, we fear the future, we cannot live in the present we have created for ourselves. And we ourselves are split into parts. Many of us feed our intellect at the expense of our emotions; others reverse the imbalance; but most of us allow our spirits to wither on the vine. And that is how we, the selves we once were or at least wanted to be, became as spiritually dry and shattered as a winter leaf.

So we need to feel the extent to which our unmanageability stems from the lack of a spiritual center. The development of our spiritual center will take time. But one place we can look for inspiration is to other people. All around us, we see people whose spiritual lives feed them—and not all of them believe in God or even in a Higher Power. Ask questions of them. Listen to their stories of how they went from a place all too familiar to us, a place of fear and despair, to a place of serenity and an active spiritual life. Learn from anyone—not just people like yourself, who believe what you believe, but people who seem to have found a spiritual life that works for them. You do not need to believe what they believe in order to see their evidence of sobriety, serenity, and spiritual development. You may disagree in the particulars, but you can see the evidence of the centrality of a spiritual life to their state of peace.

Without faith in a personified God, we may question the idea that our addiction will be taken from us. Whether or not there is a force beyond us that could or would act upon us in this way, we need to do the hard work of opening our hands and letting go of the addictive life to which we cling. That addictive life is the very thing that is killing off our bodies, minds, and souls; it is the thing that drains our spiritual lives and denies us access to our spiritual source. And so it's time to let it go.

This is a step into the unknown. We do not know what follows life after addiction. We do not know who we will be when we begin to develop as spiritual people. It is still very dark in the place where we are; we still question what comforts, what guides us as we go. But we have taken a leap of faith that a spiritual life is possible for us by opening our minds and hearts, and trusting that what is spiritual within us will guide us through the darkness and into a place where we see light. This act of faith in itself strengthens the spirit.

And if we practice this step with absolute honesty and a willingness to go where it takes us—no matter how deep a place in the soul that may be—we will find the answer in there.

We must begin our work by acknowledging our brokenness, our spiritual bankruptcy. Only by recognizing that we have come to the end of the road we were walking can we make the choice to set out on a new road. Whereas the hell of addiction was at least familiar terrain, here we do not know the way at all. Ultimately, these are Steps into a new life, and that life will require spiritual care and feeding if it is to survive.

We make a descent more than once in our lives. We reach a point where we have become spiritually drained, where we have blocked out our spiritual voice or become cut off from our spiritual source. At these moments, again, we descend.

These are the moments of winter in our lives. And in these winters, during which it seems that all is dark or even dead, we have the opportunity to go within; to study our own capacity for a faith that can endure pain or emptiness or doubt; to reach deeper for our spiritual center, listen harder for our spiritual voice, than we ever had before.

We have flickers of doubt, and we have flashes of uncertainty, and at times we fall headfirst into despair. Crisis, loss, death, tragedy, whether in our personal lives or in the larger world, cast long shadows across the sunlit path we'd like to walk.

We may doubt, during these periods, that there is meaning in human existence or that there is purpose in our individual lives. We begin to wonder whether there is anything spiritual within us or in the larger world. This sense that we may be spinning aimlessly on a rock through an indifferent universe defined by impersonal laws is lonely and frightening, and at these times it is easy to get lost in a forest of our own fear.

Many religious people would say that their faith is being tested by God at these times. And it is possible that these periods of descent, these times when our faith in meaning and purpose is called into question, are periods when our own internal selves are calling on us to strengthen our spiritual lives. Perhaps our spirits are well aware of when they need to be strengthened and tested by fire.

During these times, we have the chance to develop trust in ourselves, in our internal spiritual compass. We have the chance to learn to rely on the people we love and to more deeply experience the necessity of love and connection in our lives; we can give up the isolating notion that we are going through this life alone.

These dark moments are another chance to work Step One: to recognize areas where we are powerless and ways in which our lives have become unmanageable. Working this Step again and again will, as it did the first time we worked it, renew our acquaintance with the sound of our spiritual voice coming through the layers of our doubt, our fear, our ennui.

Whether working this Step for the first time or returning to it later in our sobriety, we are at a point of development where we are beginning or renewing a search for what has spiritual meaning for us—what we believe in, what lights our hearts on fire, what gives us strength, where we connect with other people and the world. We are looking for what is spiritually significant to us, both within and without. This is what fills our lives with meaning, what gives us purpose—our spirits, and what feeds them, and what they love.

These periods of descent allow us to again face our own smallness, our own fears, our own sense of emptiness, our own despair. These feelings are part of the human condition. And they are spiritual hungers crying out to be fed. In order to know what our spirits need, what *we* need as whole, spiritual people, we must listen. These are times when we are able to learn from the emptiness itself. We are able, when we listen and discover what we truly need, to find and make meaning for ourselves; we are able to find what may be a new direction in our lives.

Practicing Step One as we walk away from our addiction is that movement in a new direction, and it requires listening to the spiritual self. This may be the first time that we have done this in many years; some of us may never have had the opportunity or felt the need to develop our spiritual lives at all. But now it is a clear necessity if we are to move away from addiction, if we are to practice the Twelve Step program, and if we are to continue to grow.

That growth depends upon recognizing that spiritually we move outward from the center of ourselves. We find our connection with others by being aware of our spiritual core, and we are able to build meaningful relationships with them based on spiritual integrity. These inward times are a natural and necessary period in the life cycle of the soul: we are building the people we want to become, the people we want to be in the world. During these periods of darkness, we are actually developing from spiritual isolation to connection with others. Our process of finding meaning and direction for ourselves is a process of finding out how we want to contribute and what we want to give.

And so we find that by stepping into this place of darkness and by navigating its unfamiliar terrain, we come unexpectedly to a place of hope. Having recognized the insanity and spiritual brokenness of our addiction, having taken the journey to face that sense of emptiness and loss, and having come face-to-face with our own limited human nature, we come out on the other side of Step One with a deeper knowledge of ourselves as spiritual beings.

Step One is, paradoxically, both a crushing end and a beginning. The fact that we have come to recognize our powerlessness and spiritual emptiness means that we have reached a moment of spiritual awareness as well.

We would not be able to face this moment or take this Step if we did not contain a source of spiritual strength. We may not know the nature of that strength or of that spiritual self at all. But we can sense that it is there.

Having worked Step One spiritually, we arrive at Step Two with the knowledge—however tentative, however new—that we are not, in fact, spiritually empty after all. We begin to sense that there are spiritual sources that can feed us, and that there may be hope for our restoration to sanity. We can begin to believe that we will be relieved of our addiction.

Just as we know that winter will become spring, though we see no evidence of this around us, we can know that our spiritual self will emerge. We only have to wait. We wait with consciousness, attention, and awareness of what is changing within us as we still our minds and hearts long enough to listen.

We may not hear a God. But we will hear a spiritual self, an inner voice. That spiritual self is what has led us to Step One. That voice is what told us we had reached an end and needed to begin again. Even as we sit in the dark, even in this heart of winter, we find that we have already planted the seeds of faith.

CHAPTER TWO

Doubt

February

*Eventually we must face our own fears and doubts, listen to our own re-
sistance to trust, and learn from that resistance, opening ourselves to the
possibility of moving beyond it. This brings us to the question of faith, of
what we can trust when we are lost—a central question that runs through
the seasons of a spiritual life. The critical moments in life when we drop into
deep doubt are necessary moments that allow us to fully face our own fear
and to learn from it what we really want and what we need. We have come
to Step Two.*

I stepped out of the church and flinched in the blinding white light of a
cold February day in 1998. White sky, white ground, the ambient light
sharp and hard. I started to walk.

I walked and I walked. I was wearing a red dress. He had told me to wear
a red dress to his funeral. I called him a bastard and laughed. It was painful
laughter, sharp as the light. He was my best friend. He was twenty-four
and dying. We were planning the service. He said no roses. He said no
sappy hymns. He said, if we could possibly manage it, no God. We agreed
his mother might want a little God. So he said, "Okay, a little God." And
he closed his eyes and leaned back on the pillows and struggled to breathe,
but he smiled.

He died on a bitterly cold morning a few days later, before the light came
up. Through the window of his dark hospital room, the city lights looked
soft and strangely warm. We stood around his bed, sobbing and telling him

we loved him. His dying was painful. He screamed and screamed. Then he went silent and still and was dead.

I pitched face-first into my husband and slid down him to the floor. Then I realized I was on the floor. So I collected myself and stood up and went to Brian, dead on the bed. I leaned down and whispered *Thank you* in his ear.

And then there was nothing else to say, so I left. I stepped out of the hospital into that white winter light northerners know well. It's the light of the hardest season. I walked and I walked, freezing cold, my face burning with wind.

I let myself into my house. Glanced at the clock: 8 a.m. I took the bottle off the shelf. I didn't bother with a glass.

Days passed, I'm not sure how. It seemed unlikely that time should continue passing, with Brian dead. It seemed frankly absurd. It seemed equally absurd that I was tasked, now, with writing the eulogy. I sat at my desk with the bottle at my left hand and my head in my right, staring at a piece of paper and wondering how in the hell I was supposed to sum up the life of a man who hadn't had a chance to live a full life, but who lived better than anyone I'd ever known—lived wiser and kinder and with a more furious love of this world and the people in it and the fact that he got to spend any time here at all. I sat wondering if he had heard me crying *I love you* as he died. And I wondered if he'd heard me say, once he was gone, *Thank you.*

I thought it was very unlikely that he had.

But I wrote the eulogy. I wore the red dress. I stood in the pulpit in the church—a curious place to celebrate the life of a man who thought the idea of God was hogwash, but whatever—and I said my piece.

What I said was this: I doubt. I doubt the existence of a God who would be so witless as to take my dearest friend. I doubt the presence of a benevolent force. I doubt that there is anything out there that really gives a damn. Brian, of all people, should have had the chance to stick around. And so I doubt.

What I did not say was this: I am lost.

With Brian gone, it was as if the thing that had tethered me to the ground came loose and let me go. I was suddenly aware of the vastness of things, the smallness of myself, the brutal brevity of life. I felt as if I were spinning through space, the only sound an echo of my own voice.

I wanted comfort. I wanted reassurance that there was something else, something out there, something keeping Brian in a place where he could be found. I could not find this comfort. So I drank.

And it was no more comfort than an absent God.

—

This year, February rushes in hard on a cruel wind. It's this time of year that takes northerners down. The loveliness of early winter has gone, and what's left is the stripped-bare landscape: black trees, white ground, white sky. It's been a while since we've seen even the winter sun.

I am standing knee-deep in the snow, staring down at my garden, or the snow-buried place where my garden should be. May be. Really, if all things go according to natural law, the place where my garden *will* be, come spring. There are bulbs tucked into the frozen earth, doing whatever it is that bulbs do in their preparations for growth. There are plants that bloom year after year, their cut-back black and wheat-colored stalks just barely visible above the snow. And I know, technically, that they should bloom.

But this year I have my doubts.

It's very weird. My friends with gardens laugh at me, but I persist in my anxiety, certain that my garden won't come up. I'm convinced that this year, when the snow melts, it will leave mud and then soft dirt and then . . . nothing. No green shoots, no bulbs bursting and sending up their many-colored blooms. My friends tell me this is the order of things: things sleep all winter, then bloom. It happens every year. But my hydrangeas, I'm pretty sure, are good and dead, killed off by an early frost last fall. And I know al-most for a fact that all my perennials will fail. So here I stand, knee-deep in snow, staring at the place where my garden should be, and I am full of doubt.

The year Brian died, I was quite sure spring would not come, at least for me, because I could not conceive of a way to survive without him in the world. I was half-crazed with grief; I truly believed I would die of the pain. I couldn't see how any other outcome was possible. And so I spent February staring out the window, drinking, waiting for the pain to finally break me in half.

It didn't. Obviously. Obviously, I survived. Obviously, spring came, and when it did, I was genuinely shocked. How could it be spring if Brian was dead? What sort of unlikely notion had the universe taken to go and make it *spring*?

But spring came again the following year, and again, and again, and the universe kept operating in the way that it does, bringing winter, bringing spring. And as the years went by, I began to feel less sharply the loss of Brian and more powerfully the myriad gifts he'd brought into my life.

The doubt that there was *anything out there* began to fade. I didn't believe in God any more than I had before; but I became aware of my own sense that the universe *does* operate on certain principles, and while we cannot deny that there is random tragedy and pain, we also cannot deny that there is random goodness and grace. The gift of Brian in my life was as unlikely and shocking as his death; and though I had lost him, I had been graced with him first. And the things he brought me endured.

I wasn't able, when he died, to find the grace and gratitude for his life in the sea of pain at his death. I went looking for a simple savior; a bottle sufficed.

But those were other days. I know better now how to handle loss, accept doubt, live with the unknown. I learned to wait for spring. Spring came. Sobriety brought it.

This year, as I tromp through my garden, full of doubt, scowling at the snow, I suddenly pause. A flicker of red wings and a flurry of snow scattering from the lilac branches: a cardinal. He sits very still. We watch each other awhile, two creatures who have the dumb persistence to live in the north, muddle through the winter, and, sometimes stubbornly, sometimes peacefully, wait.

—

As powerful and painful as the admission of powerlessness is for all of us, the next stage of this spiritual process—where we are asked to believe that we can be restored to sanity by a "Power greater than ourselves"—causes nonbelievers to stumble in a way that the First Step may not have done. Were we willing to admit, finally, that our lives were out of control, that we were spiritually bankrupt, that we were desperate for some kind of healing solution to the pain in our lives? Yes. We could admit that. But having been leveled in that way, having seen our spiritual destitution and emptiness for what they were, having reached that nadir of the heart's life cycle, we are now faced with what seems an impossible task. It seems that we are being asked to believe in a God. And many of us simply don't.

But the Step says nothing about God. It asks us to believe in "a Power greater than ourselves."

I'll grant you that capitalizing "Power" makes it look like a stand-in word for "God." But it's not. It's not a stand-in for anything; it means what it says. Can you believe in something bigger than yourself? Are there things in this universe more powerful than you? There are sure as hell things more powerful than me. I am simply not the be-all and end-all of the universe. So yes, I am willing to believe in a power, or *many* powers, greater than myself.

But what are they? What is their nature, and what is their relationship to me? *Is* there a relationship between those powers and myself? This is a pressing question, because we are also being asked to believe that this power or these powers have the capacity to restore us to sanity.

And that's where we may get into trouble. While I don't find it hard to see that I am not the most powerful thing in the universe, I *do* have a hard time understanding what interest some universal power may take in my very small life. I picture myself as a speck of a thing, tumbling end over end through space. While I am aware that there are powerful things all around me, I do not trust that those things have any *personal* relationship to me at all.

Many believers in God trust that there is the possibility of a personal relationship with that God. Nonbelievers question this, and may question it so strongly that it can stop them on their spiritual journey. They may run up against the existential question, *Who or what is out there?* come to the conclusion that there is nothing, and give up. But the problem here is not the answer—it is the question. To ask who or what exists "out there" is to continue a search for a spirituality outside ourselves, a personified spiritual source we assume must come from some great beyond. The spiritual journey we are on, however, is one that takes place here, in this world, in this human community, in this spiritual self. And so we can't keep asking the same questions; we need to reframe the very basis of what it is we are trying to understand.

This is why it's essential to take a serious look at our beliefs about powers greater than ourselves and begin to develop an idea of what powers exist that we *can* relate to, here and now, in this world. These are the things that we can trust to restore us to sanity. They do exist, and we will be restored. But this Step is one of the more spiritually challenging ones for nonbelievers—and, as such, when we work it carefully, it will spark enormous spiritual growth.

The first stage in that growth is the experience of *doubt,* the spiritual issue at work in us right now. Whether or not we believe in a Higher Power, all recovering people struggle with some measure of doubt. Nonbelievers doubt the very existence of a power greater than themselves; we all have doubts as to whether such a power can or will restore us to sanity; many of us have doubts about whether the Twelve Step program itself will work in our lives; and many of us, still newly finding our spiritual selves, doubt whether we are spiritual creatures at all.

This is why the spiritual emptiness we just faced may seem, at first, to deepen even further now. We are flooded with doubt and feel ourselves reaching for some kind of assurance, some kind of certainty, an answer to the sea of questions that roils within us. People often say they wish they *could* believe in God, just so they could have *something* in which to place their faith—something that would make a spiritual source clear, easily and readily defined.

This desire for certainty is a longing that seems to be part and parcel of the human condition: We want to know. We want to be sure. We want to feel certain and safe. But letting go of the belief that we *must* have that certainty is a part of spiritual growth. Letting go, and learning to accept doubt, allows us to go deeper into our spiritual core and learn better who we are and what we believe.

Doubt is at the very heart of the spiritual experience. Without it, we would never ask the hard questions about the nature of our existence: Why are we here? How did we get here? What are our origins? What is our purpose, what are our ends? These are spiritual questions, asked by spiritual people, and they lead to spiritual growth.

The spiritual growth made possible by doubt is at the center of a spiritual life. Doubt forces us to undergo a number of spiritual acts, and the most powerful is this: When we doubt, we learn to accept that we may not ever know. When we question, we learn to accept that there may be no answer. When we shout our doubt out into the universe, we learn to accept that we may be met with a silence we do not know how to read.

This is not, on the face of it, the comfort we crave. It is not clear and present evidence that we will be restored to sanity. It is instead evidence of what we may greatly fear: our own smallness, our insignificance in the scheme of things. This is where we ask ourselves, again and again, Is there even anything out there?

And this is where we must wait. Waiting through doubt teaches us enormous spiritual strength. It gives us the strength to go on—through struggle, through joy, through recovery, through our daily lives—even though we do not know how to name or describe a power or powers greater than ourselves. And the paradox is this: to accept this not-knowing—to accept doubt, a lack of certainty—is to accept the very nature of life as it is. In accepting doubt, unanswered questions, and unknowing, we accept life on life's terms.

In times of doubt, we need to get out of our heads and into our hearts, our spiritual selves. This is unfamiliar territory for many of us. We are used to crashing through life headfirst. But if we are to accept the feeling of uncertainty, face our own spiritual questions, and come to terms with the fact that the answers may not take the form of logical proofs, we must reach deeper in ourselves than simple intellect allows us to go. We need to familiarize ourselves here with our nascent sense of spiritual self, beginning the process of integrating the split-off parts of our interior lives—mind, emotion, spirit—toward the end of becoming whole people, and healed.

The Greek root of the word *logical* is *logos*, which means "name." We want a name for the thing in which we are to believe. If there is something greater than us, we demand to know what it is called. It's true that the phrase "Came to believe in a Power greater than ourselves" is highly unsatisfying to our logical, naming brains—What Power? What is it? What is it called? What am I being asked to believe *in*?

But perhaps there is no *thing,* no *it* that will satisfy our passion for naming and knowing. Perhaps it really is simply a "power," which is nothing if not shapeless, amorphous, beyond intellectual absolutes. Perhaps it exists entirely within the human mind and heart. We are not being asked to believe in anything specific. The suggestion of the second Step is that we *come* to believe—over time, in a process entirely personal and without rules—in something much simpler than we try to make it: something bigger than us.

So we can call it whatever we like, and we can conceptualize it as anything we want. What matters is that our spirits respond to our sense of it. This is where making a doorknob your Higher Power may not be spiritually sufficient. But that does not mean that you are being asked to make the leap from a doorknob to a God. Call it the feeling of love that connects us. Call it the creative force that drives us to transform. Call it our energy. Call it our capacity to give. Call it grace, or even divinity, something that allows for those things to exist within us as individuals and between us each time we connect.

Because that is what we are after here: a belief in whatever it is that works in our lives, in our hearts, here and now. We are not after an explanation of the origins of the universe or an answer to what happens when we die. We will not answer those things. No one has, at least to my satisfaction, and perhaps no one ever will. Right now we are not casting about for certain answers to universal unknowns. Rather, we are working a practical program of rebuilding our lives, and this stage, as challenging as it may be to us intellectually, is actually very simple. Is something bigger than I am, and more powerful? Most things, actually, are more powerful. Good and evil, love and hatred, creative and destructive energy, wonder and awe, pain and suffering—while I *contain* all of these things, while all humans do, their cumulative force in the larger world is more powerful than I am myself.

When I stop trying to find the key to universal mysteries, I find it's much easier to accept the notion that there's something larger and more powerful than me. The trick, really, is getting comfortable with not knowing exactly what that is and having faith in it anyway.

The desire to clearly and definitively understand powers greater than ourselves is common, and probably futile. The very nature of spirit and spirituality defies language and explanation. This is due in great part to the fact that spirit and spirituality are *experienced* differently by each one of us; we do not have a common language for how the spirit feels when it is hungry or when it is fulfilled. We are often wordless in the realm of spiritual experience. And that's fine; we are not being asked to state our position on the matter. We are being asked to come to believe—on our own time, in our own way—that we can be healed by these myriad forces that surround us and that we contain.

The way toward a personal understanding of spiritual experience may be something other than understanding an external God or force of any kind. The way may be instead to know your own spiritual self more deeply— what you need, what feeds you, what you thrill to, what darkens your heart, what makes you feel empty or whole. Because it is through a clear sense of our own spiritual nature, gifts, and needs that we will be able to connect spiritually with the world. And that is what we are trying to do: develop a spiritual relationship with the world in which we live, a relationship we've been starving for since the beginning of our addiction. So the pressing spiritual questions for us are not *What's out there? Where are we from? Where will we go?* but rather *How do we live?*

And we need to find that out. Right now, we are acknowledging that we have not lived in a way that kept us spiritually alive or spiritually connected to the people around us or to the greater world. We are acknowledging the insanity of living in a kind of isolation and spiritual death. And we are coming to believe that something can restore us to the sanity of a spiritually fulfilling life.

So can that something—that power greater than ourselves—guide us? Comfort us? Tell us how to live? Are we able to believe that? Some are, some are not. Some of us feel that those are powers of a personified God in which we do not believe. The range of what and how we believe is vast. And while we cannot always see the powers greater than ourselves as personally interested in our lives in the ways a traditional God is believed to be, it is possible for us to believe that something *can* teach us how to live.

Believing as we do—that vast range of beliefs—we may come to understand that we need to find guidance, comfort, and support, in this world, in the things that move our spirits here and now. We turn first to others whose lives we admire and who have the spiritual serenity we crave; and, as we become ever more closely attuned to our own spiritual voice, we begin to trust our own wisdom as well.

Can that inner wisdom be called a "Higher Power"? Maybe not. But the spiritual life within us, the spiritual wisdom we learn from others, and the spiritual connections we create as we move toward sanity are certainly powers greater than our minds and understanding, and greater than our limited selves. So at some point we can, in fact, recognize that there is a power greater than ourselves: it is *all that is beyond our limited knowledge and control.* That massive, infinite web of forces is far greater than I.

All we have to do is recognize our limits—that we are not all—and then we are prepared to turn our attention to how we live. To today. To our action in this world.

The spiritual realm is not the ethereal beyond our lived experience. It is our experience, lived fully and well. We are not looking for a theology or a God. We do not have to understand or name how we became. We only have to understand that we *are* and that we must *act.* Part of spiritual experience is an awareness of lived experience as something we need to attend to, not only with our minds but with spirit as well. A spiritual transformation takes place as we deepen that awareness of our daily lives, our actions, our relationships—and this deepening awareness *is* a return to sanity.

With deepening awareness of ourselves as spiritual, we begin to act from a moral center that may have gotten lost along the course of our addictive lives. We begin to make choices and take action from a place in ourselves that knows responsibility, love, respect, wonder, willingness, and gratitude. It is this spiritual voice in ourselves that we begin to listen to when we need to know what to think, feel, or do; and it is this spiritual part of ourselves that is capable of connection with others and with the world.

Early in sobriety, we may listen long and hard and still feel we're hearing nothing but the echo of our own minds. But the process of our return to sanity brings us into connection with others and brings us to a peaceful place in ourselves.

So we learn to wait—for words and examples of guidance from others, for inspiration, for our spiritual wisdom to surface, for our spiritual selves to find their way. We wait for a deeper understanding of our own spiritual center and for the strengthening of our connection with the spiritual life of the world. Living each day with awareness and spiritual engagement, we return to the sane and humbling realization that we are very small, that we control very little, that we know even less—and that powers greater than ourselves can lead us back to a sane, serene, and spiritual life, if we are willing to wait.

The question of how these greater powers can restore us to sanity is one that will be answered differently in each individual's life. But there is plenty of evidence that sanity *can* be restored and that it *does* require us to reach for a spiritual source *of our own understanding.* If we could have done it on our own, we would have, every last one of us. We could not. But there are millions of people living sober and strongly spiritual lives, each one different from the next, no two people requiring the same concept of spirituality or powers greater than themselves. They have found within themselves and in the larger world a spiritual source. They are all the evidence we need to believe this can happen for us.

And we begin to understand in Step Two that we are our own proof of spiritual power. When we take this Step, we must acknowledge that there is something driving us forward to sanity, toward sobriety, toward an entirely new life.

That something is our spiritual selves. We may doubt a Higher Power; we may doubt meaning; we may doubt origins or ends. But we cannot argue with the hard fact of our lives: We have survived, we want to survive, and we trust—at least a little, or we would not be here—that there is more to us than our addiction allowed us to believe. We are no longer driven by a substance, a craving, a habit, a fear. We are driven by a deeper desire, even when that desire leads us to a place of incredible doubt.

Recognizing this, we stumble upon the spiritual gift of Step Two: we see the first flickerings of hope.

As we move through our lives in recovery, we encounter doubt again and again. It's part of our human nature and part of the human experience. We come up against moments that send us spiraling into uncertainty—about the meaning of our lives, the meaning of events in our lives and in the world, about our own purpose as people, our own abilities, our capacity for strength in the face of struggle, even our own capacity for love. We doubt our worth. We doubt things in which we have previously had great faith.

It may be a loss we experience, of a loved one, or of something like our belief in the basic goodness of life and of people. It may be a crisis in our lives or an enormous tragedy in the world. Doubt can surface at moments of change or transition, when a period of our lives comes to an end and another begins—we may doubt the future, and the unknown.

We may feel, at these times, our spiritual selves rising up in anger, in confusion, and in grief. We may cast about for something in which we *can* have faith, something that can give us a sense of security and certainty, as we did for years with our addiction. We may feel our sense of serenity slip away and our spiritual selves beginning to close down.

And this is what we can't allow to happen. During these periods of doubt—and they will come—we cannot allow our spiritual lives to go un-attended. We can choose the opposite of that, and that choice allows for enormous spiritual growth. We can choose to experience doubt, the loss of faith, as a spiritual moment that can teach us more about how to live as spiritual people.

So rather than running from doubt, shutting down our spirits and hearts, or reaching for quick certainty, we can use doubt as a spiritual practice. We can wait. We wait for our tangled emotions to unknot themselves; we wait for our troubled or angry or grieving spirits to let their sorrow go. We wait for the humility to recognize our limitations and our lack of control, for this humility will bring us peace while we wait. We wait for answers; we wait for clarity; we wait for faith to return in its own time. And it will.

Faith—whatever faith we have lost—may return in an entirely different form. We may find ourselves believing in an entirely different way than we did before. We may find ourselves transformed through the spiritual practice of waiting in doubt.

This practice of strengthening ourselves, our spirits, such that they have the capacity to endure the spiritual struggle of doubt, is a practice we need as we move through the Steps. We have learned that we can "come to believe"—that it is a process, that it takes time, that it comes and goes. We've learned that it requires attentiveness to our spiritual selves. It does not require that we believe in any specific creed or God; it requires that we live our lives from our spiritual center and reach out from that place to connect with others and with the world.

As we practice this Step, we build a foundation for a spiritual life. We feel more acutely the spiritual drive in ourselves toward a new way of being. And we find ourselves with an ability to believe that we will be restored to sanity, to serenity, and to peace.

We also find ourselves at the doorway to Step Three. Through the practice of waiting and the acceptance of not-knowing, we have begun to develop what we will need to work the next Step: willingness. We have been growing in willingness throughout our work on Step Two; now we have the willingness we need to turn over our will and our lives.

CHAPTER THREE

Letting Go

March

We must let go of our vise grip on the notion of control and realize that the desire for control is born of fear. When we can't place our trust in a God, the very fact of not-knowing allows us to accept our lack of control, our lack of certainty, and opens the door to full surrender. As addicts, we have lived with a delusion of control, cutting us off from both ourselves and others, from our spiritual wisdom and theirs. Surrendering to our own lack of knowing is a vital practice. We have come to Step Three.

I've gone north and west into the prairie, near the North Dakota border, to watch the lake thaw.

This doesn't sound like a particularly exhilarating experience, maybe. But to me it is. Every morning as the sun comes up, I pull on my boots and coat over my pajamas and walk down to the edge of the ice. I tap my toe along the thinning crust of it and watch the water, clean and crystal clear, spring out onto the frozen sand.

Well, yesterday I walked down there and put my boot straight through. I was feeling cluttered and jangled and too much was in my head, and I marched down to the water and stomped on the ice. It was surprisingly satisfactory. My foot thus soaked with freezing water, I sloshed back up to the house, feeling far more peaceful than I had before.

This is my grandmother's house, and this is her porch where I sit bundled against the wind that whips over the lake and sends the thin remaining snow spinning in whorls. This is her small town where I've been coming since I was a girl. This is the view she looked at for I don't know how many years, the same view every day: the dock, in summertime the boats tied to it; in winter the ice-fishing shacks that dot the lake. This is her ancient chair where I now sit, where she sat writing letters, years of letters in her tight, back-slanted hand, a look of calm and order on her face, a Parliament burning in the ashtray, and an all-encompassing sense one got in her presence that all was well, and would be well, and was in place.

My grandmother kept a journal for sixty years. When she died, I sat on the floor of my apartment and read this chronicle of a life of days. It stunned me. Not because of the earth-shattering insights it held or the breadth of philosophical thought it contained. Because of the opposite. It did not record her grand notions or even her thoughts. It recorded her life.

Her life was a practice. I would say it was a spiritual practice, whether she intended it to be or not. I'd imagine it was not an exciting life for anyone else. Reading these journals was not thrilling; it was quiet and meditative and strangely hypnotic, and as I read, I left the room I was in and entered her world. In the litany of things cooked and sewn and ironed and washed, I found myself looking around at the precise details of her house, her porch, the view of the lake, the walk down Main Street and back. In the precise dating of events—my father's birth, the day my aunt hit him on the head with a hammer, the time she shocked us all and took a trip around the world, my grandfather's death—I saw a life precisely observed and very consciously lived.

There's a Buddhist saying: "Before enlightenment, I chopped wood and carried water. After enlightenment, I chopped wood and carried water." That, I think, is what my grandmother did. She lived fully, within the scope of her world. We may say it was a narrow world. We may wonder if she felt confined or bored. We may suspect—and I do—that there was much left unsaid in these journals, much that she erased before she even wrote it down. But there is a quality of peace to what she does say, as there was a quality of peace about her. Here, some might wonder if she believed in God and whether her sense of peace and order came from her knowledge of God's presence and following of God's will. I don't know if she believed in God; he's never mentioned in the journals, but then neither is my grandfather and I know he existed. She went to church, but then that was what one did; it seems entirely possible to me that she took God as a simple fact, as my grandfather was a fact, and neither of them concerned her too much one way or the other.

So I don't know if she ever sat out here on her porch and wrestled with the question of God. I don't know if she came up in the negative or the affirmative as to whether one was at work in her life. I don't know if she felt doubt. Most of us do—doubt of ourselves, doubt of others, of our lives, of whether there is something running the show, of whether we're alone. I don't know what or if she doubted.

I do doubt she ever felt so cluttered and noisy and jangled that she put her boot through the ice. As soon as I did it, I could just hear her saying in alarm, "Well. My stars!"

But there are days I do feel that way, and I am beginning to know that it is because I hold on. I fight. I resist. It doesn't even matter what I resist; there is simply something in me that tends to resist things as they are. I have been fighting since I was very small. And I believe that my addiction was a response, in some measure, to the fact that the fight was futile, and I could not tolerate that fact. I couldn't tolerate the fact that I did not control the world. I could not, or would not, learn to accept it.

The practice of acceptance isn't something that comes easily to very many of us. I think it's in the nature of the human—at least many humans—to think that we can control virtually everything, and that belief leads to a constant fight against the fact that we can't. The fight is exhausting, but we seem to be convinced that we can win. We place our faith in ourselves, in our minds, in our firm belief that we are in charge. When we find that we aren't, we feel out of control and that scares us, so we fight. We fight other people; we fight change; we fight sameness; we fight ourselves. It reminds me of the absurd lesson I learned in fifth-grade English class, which was that all literature could be boiled down to three tales we tell: Man Against Nature, Man Against Man, and Man Against Himself. It's a very silly theory. It certainly doesn't sum up the entirety of literature. But it does tell one story, and that one is common enough: we fight.

And there are fights worth the effort. There are ways the world works now in which it should not work and ways it has worked in the past that needed to change, and the people who fought for that change brought necessary things to the way we operate as a human community. I'm not saying it's a good plan to simply ignore that which isn't right—isn't right in a very true and real sense—but that isn't usually what we fight. The causes we take up in our minds aren't often noble. They are often very small. I look back at the tiny wars I've waged in my life and wonder what I was doing. It seems an awful lot of wasted effort to have fought for things that in the end didn't matter at all, and in the end I could never have changed.

We fight, I think, out of fear. And there is so much that we fear. We fear that we will lose what we have, will not get what we need, will not have enough, will never be who we think we should be. We fear we will not be happy. We fear we will not be content.

But the people who are content, I think, do not fight.

When I was a girl, I had a book of folktales that I loved and lugged around with me everywhere. Nearly forty years later, I still remember this one: A man was unhappy. He decided to search for the key to happiness; he decided to search for a happy man, and when he found this man, he would borrow his shirt. He went to a rich man, but even in his shirt made of gold thread, the rich man was not happy. He went to a man with knowledge, but he in his scholar's cloak was not happy either. He went to the handsomest young man in the land, but even in the finest fashions, even with his beauty and youth, the young man was not happy in the least. And then, one day, walking along the road, he saw a man singing. And the man who sought happiness was crestfallen. The happy man wore no shirt.

I think what my grandmother knew was that though her world was small, it was her world, it was where she lived, and it was enough. It was simply enough. It was her life, and it would proceed as it did, without her input, without her attempts to control its passage, or its seasons, or the things that went away and returned and then were gone again.

For those of us who do not know a God, there seems sometimes to be nothing in which to place our trust. No higher authority, no comforter, no assurance that there is always something more waiting for us out there. So I think we must learn to trust the world, this world we are in, here and now.

One day, my grandmother was sitting with two other women on her porch. One woman, Clarice, had just lost her husband. The other woman said to her, "Well, dear, he's in a better place." Clarice looked at her in disbelief. "Are you kidding?" she said. "Kid, just look at that lake!"

As I write this, the watery light of dawn is coming up over the frozen lake. I'm waiting for the loons to return. I don't know when loons fly north. But if I sit here long enough, I expect the ice will melt—even if I do not check its progress every day—and the loons will come skidding into the water and send their strange laughter out into the still-cold April air.

But for that, I have to wait.

—

The doubt and fear that often overtake me come from a desire to know more than I can know. To control more than it is my purview to control and to control it by knowing it, intellectually mastering it, neatly delineating it into questions I ask and answers I have. I take on the universe and try to make it human-sized, one-person-sized, self-sized. I persist in the notion that I can hold it all in my two hands, grip it tightly, make it mine.

To trust is to let go.

Trust is the answer to doubt. We have a habit of thinking one must trust *in* something, as if trust were not a perfectly solid thing, a perfectly good noun, unto itself. I think it's probably in our nature to cast about for something in which to place our trust or, to use another word, our faith; we seem to very much want to place our faith in a known quantity, a God or a creed or a code or a logic or something we see as having the answers, as *being* the answers, to any question we might ask.

Instead, here we are with our heads and hearts full of questions to which we do not, and I believe cannot, know the answers. We're human. We are by definition bound by our own perceptions, our own limitations. The human animal is remarkable for its curiosity and for its limitations alike. It's astonishing that we can think up infinite questions to which we want answers and yet have means with which to answer very few. This quandary is, I believe, one of the best and most infuriating aspects of being a person.

Infuriating for obvious reasons—we want desperately to know, because we think if we know we will feel less adrift, less scared, less lost. But I say this quandary is also one of the best aspects because it forces us to come to grips with what and who we are.

To face one's own tininess in the context of all that exists is a terrifying prospect, if we really allow ourselves to think about it. Here we are, in our chairs, on a spinning planet in a sky, orbiting a ball of flame. Here we are, one body of precise weight and measure, attached by invisible but actual forces to this square of earth, which is what we know at this moment, and all we know.

It is also all we have to know. Here on our square we are tiny in the face of the cosmos, the very notion of the infinite beyond our true comprehension, but here on our square we are also *alive*. We are living and breathing and thinking and knowing and not-knowing and perceiving and feeling as we feel right now.

This square of earth is not all that is. It is not all we are aware of or all we ever need to think about. But it is all we can fully and truly *know*. And it is where we *are*. And it is where we must *live*. It is what grounds us in our questioning. It is where we stand when we look up at the reeling stars. It is what gives us a sense of soundness and certainty, even as we doubt.

Being here, living now, recognizing our smallness, is a spiritual practice. It allows us to be at peace with our humanity. It humbles us and grants us permission to fumble, and not know, and fail, and also to take pleasure in the small triumphs of our days.

Humility is an essential component of a spiritual life. The word *humility* is too often seen as a negative, when in fact a lack of humility—arrogance, grandiosity, judgment, superiority, all of the unpleasant things we're prone to anyway—burdens us with the need to feel that we are masters of our lives and all that they contain. This is in fact an impossible burden; the need to be right, to feel we're in control, is a state of anxiety that cannot be eased, because we cannot ever fully and finally *be* right about or in control of all things at all times.

Realizing at last that we can relax and be wrong is an enormous relief. Not only *can* we be wrong; we can rest in the certainty that we will be. We don't have to know everything, and we don't have to try to manage everyone in our lives so they behave to our liking, and we don't have to stand behind the planet and push it to make sure it turns as we think it should turn. It won't. They won't. We can trust that we will mess up, that we will misbehave, and that the planet will continue to spin quite independently of our wills.

As to our wills. Truculent, stubborn, bossy, and frankly childish, or perhaps I am only speaking of my will. But I have found willfulness to be a feature observable in many people, and behind willfulness is the belief that we must have our way. It's not complex. It isn't something to be particularly proud of, although we are encouraged at every turn to act according to our will. It's a regrettable habit we have of thinking we are entitled to have all we want.

This isn't the way the world works. We even *know* this isn't the way the world works. We know, in theory, that there is disappointment, there is loss, there is pain, that we are not the only ones who want what we want when we want it—there is the whole rest of humanity to consider, of course, but we persist. And to persist is to put ourselves in opposition to everyone, and everything, all the time.

Humility is a means of bringing ourselves back to reality. And it is a means of finding a great deal of the peace that has eluded us for so long. We are egged on constantly to want and pursue at all costs, more, and more, and more. More money, more success, more approval, more security, more proof of love. But part of a spiritual life is learning to look beyond the superficial, to reach deeper in ourselves for the wisdom we do contain. And that wisdom, when we're listening, tells us that we are more than grasping, demanding, will-driven creatures who *want.*

Humility is also a means of bringing ourselves back to ourselves. It grounds us in the bodies we have, in the place where we are at this moment, to work with the mixture of gifts and flaws we possess at this time. We are capable of evolution and transformation, when we are aware of these gifts and flaws; we can become more whole, and more spiritual, and more capable of living in peace. But when we begin to believe we are in control, we stop evolving, and we get stuck.

Stuck in the belief that the course and outcome of our lives are things we can foresee and know, we shut our eyes to the lives we are actually leading, moment by moment, close off our hearts from necessary seasons of joy and pain, and close our minds to the possibility that there is more to learn, more to the world and its workings, than we can ever understand. That fact should, by all reason, cause us wonder; instead it scares us. That we are small in the face of things that are vast, that we are powerless in the face of things we cannot control, that there *are* seasons of joy and pain that will come and go without our permission, that life is as it is—this sends us running for certainty and security and the solitary comfort of the closed-off self. We hide in the fantasy that our will is enough to run our lives and that our lives are even in our hands.

Or it sends us running for a drink. Name your poison. Any illusion will do.

When we're shut down in this way—by addiction, by fighting, by attempts to control, by what the Big Book aptly calls "self-will run riot"—we have no space in ourselves for spiritual growth or awareness. And we need that space. Without it, our spirits wither, and we become people who cannot give, who cannot receive, who cannot see themselves or others clearly. Our hearts become rigid and cannot love. We have no ability to really experience the life we are living. And we have no ability to accept.

Humility makes room in us for acceptance, and without that acceptance, we will never know peace. But it's true that what we have to accept is no small thing: we have to accept that we are limited beings with limited power and very limited knowledge. And accepting this is true surrender. It is letting go.

I like the word *surrender* about as much as the next controlling person, which is basically not at all. I hear it, and I feel myself start to fight. Surrender to what? To whom? What for? Who says?

Which is more or less to say: What? I'm not in charge?

In fact, no. Much as my inner two-year-old would like to think I am.

Then who is?

Those of us who do not believe in a God as such, and who may have trouble conceiving of a Higher Power at all, spend an inordinate amount of time on the question of what the Higher Power is, in which we do not believe—or what the Higher Power is in which we *could* believe—and we get ourselves quite tangled up.

The undoing of this tangle is, for the nonbeliever, a monumental task. I think in some part of ourselves, we believe that if we think about it hard enough, we will come up with a notion of a Higher Power *outside ourselves* that will work for us. In short, we keep waiting for God. We keep arguing with ourselves about whether such a thing exists. And this argument, like so many, is a circular one: we will keep coming back and back and back to the fact that we *don't know*. We don't know what powers outside ourselves may or may not exist. Some people claim to know, and who am I to say? Maybe they know, and maybe they're right. But for the purposes of my own spirituality, it is far more useful to recognize the limitations of my knowledge; to humble myself, not before a deity, but simply to *be humble;* to surrender, again, not to a God but simply *to surrender;* and to accept. Not accept certain facts; but simply to train myself in the *practice of acceptance.*

The trouble with the language commonly used to discuss spirituality is that it's structured along subject/object lines: there is always a surrendering *to* X, turning it over *to* X, an acceptance *of* X, a trusting *of* X, a gratitude *for* X.

What if we just surrendered, accepted, and were grateful?

This, to me, is the spiritual practice of letting go.

We need to let go of so many things, and each of us has our own unique things to which we cling, that there's no way to make a list of what must be let go. It would be awfully handy if there were such a list; it would give us a sense of a task we could undertake, complete, and be done. But that's the antithesis of the process of letting go, which is ongoing, and the practice of letting go, which we undertake again each day. That's the nature of a spiritual practice: it never ends, and that is its beauty, because as we continue to practice, we continue to grow.

But one of the things I have had to let go is the need to know the nature of origins and ends. I remember lying awake as a teenager, staring at the ceiling and wondering, Where did this all come from? Who or what set it in motion? What is its purpose? Where does it go? What is *my* purpose, and how do I know?

Part of my process of spiritual growth involves letting go of the need for absolute answers as to the origins of the universe, which I'm unlikely to solve; and as to the purpose of life, which is too broad a question for my particular mind; and as to what's at the end of the road we're all on, which even the broadest minds cannot begin to guess. It isn't that these things don't have meaning; it isn't even that I can't let them tumble over each other in my head when they wander in. It's just that I cannot demand—of whom would I demand them?—absolute answers. I have to accept that I will find no certainty here. Much as I like, and too often crave, certainty and reassurance, I have to accept that sometimes there is none to be found—and that, too, allows me spiritual growth. Living with my own uncertainty, like living with my own pain or gladness or frustration or any other thing that comes my way, is a practice of accepting the spiritual state of being alive.

The desire for absolute answers to these very human questions is reflective of the idea that we can know. We may *want* to know. I would like very much to know where the universe came from, what I'm supposed to do with my life, and where I'm headed when I die. But I accept that I *don't* know, and won't, and so I have no choice but to live *now*, unknowing, and with as much wonder as I can remember to have in my heart.

Wanting absolute answers also comes from the desire to be given a sense of safety—granted this sense of safety—by something outside ourselves. And this is reflective of the belief that *spirituality* comes from outside oneself, that the spiritual is another realm, that there is in fact a Higher Power separate from our own beings, which cannot be experienced until the absolutes are understood. But the opposite could well be true. The absolute answers we might come up with could just as easily be limitations; produced by human perception, they may be not much more than projections of ourselves, our needs, our desires, our fears, our way of seeing. Some would hold that God made man in His image; I'm not the first to suggest that the opposite might be true.

And still, many of us persuade ourselves of other certainties, other absolutes. We find ourselves an answer. *The* answer. We believe we've found it—that one central fact or theory, that religion or political view or funda-mentalist dictum—the answer, the thing that saves us from our own anxi-ety and the angst we feel at the perpetual ambiguity of life. We like our answer. Many of us flit from answer to answer to answer for years—and many of us, as addicts, behaved very much as if our addiction was all the answer we'd ever need.

So what I am here suggesting—that there is no final answer, no proof, no absolutely knowable truth, not in the human experience—puts us in a place that may not immediately feel comfortable. It may not feel warm, en-veloping, comforting, in the way a final answer, especially a religious figure conceived as comforter personified, might feel. It may, for some of us, leave the pain and loneliness we have felt in our spiritual crisis undiluted, at first.

But I am not *only* suggesting spiritual growth through an acceptance of unknowing. I am suggesting, at the very core of it, that spirituality is to be found here in this world—the comfort we require, the spiritual nourish-ment we need—in the form of the community we develop, upon which we depend, and to which we dedicate all that we have. This, too, comforts us and guides us as we move through our lives.

It's extremely difficult, though, to stop thinking in terms of higher powers and other realms, even when we utterly lack the belief that they exist. It's hard to stop thinking of ourselves as requiring a spiritual authority in order to be spiritual beings. It's hard to think of having a spiritual self that was not placed in our bodies by an external spiritual source. We have very little lan-guage for such a thing. It's especially challenging when we've been raised in a family or a culture that is predominantly religious in its spiritual thinking. Religious language sometimes leaves little room for interpretation and little room, in some cases, to understand one's own spiritual beliefs.

The Twelve Step programs can sometimes feel spiritually limiting in this very way. The Big Book says at one point, "Either God is everything or else He is nothing" (page 53). Well, that's an awfully rigid way of seeing things. I suppose one can answer it however one chooses, but I believe we need to let go of the need to be sure. Surety is not a spiritual practice; it is an intellec-tual position and closes the heart and the mind to what might be. Another passage in the Big Book: "We read wordy books and indulge in windy arguments, thinking we believe this universe needs no God to explain it" (page 49). This, I suppose, would be one of those books. The Big Book goes on, "Were our contentions true, it would follow that life originated out of nothing, means nothing, and proceeds nowhere" (page 49).

That doesn't actually follow. But we are trained to think in religious terms, and finding our own nonreligious spiritual language takes time. And there are questions that nag at us as we try to find our way to a spirituality that allows for our lack of a God: Without God, what gives guidance? How do we choose, how do we act? On what principles, if they are not handed down to us by God? What does it mean to not answer to a God? To whom are we responsible, if not to only ourselves? What can we trust, recognizing our own flawed perception? What wisdom of our own, and what wisdom of others?

And then there is the very amorphous question of whether there is a purpose to all that exists. Well, here's my two cents. The universe may have purpose, it may not; it may just be a thing that occurred. But *we* have purpose. We may not have *one* purpose, and we may not have a purpose granted to us from some outside force—there may be no destiny, no fate, no meant-to-be. But perhaps our purpose is, for the time being, to be human, to live on this earth and in this human community, to receive something from it, and to give something back.

Therein, I think, lies the answer to most of the questions raised above: We may be "alone" in the universe, if we are looking for a cosmic, personified force. But we are by no means alone in this world. Here, there is a community of which we are a part, whether we like it or not, and we don't always like it. But we are always answerable to it. We always carry a responsibility to be a decent and contributing member of it; we likewise carry the responsibility to become our own better selves so that we can give more than we take. How do we choose, how do we act, on what principles? Turning our attention to our lived experience, we come upon the need for a deeper understanding of our ethics, our morals, our beliefs; and these things can only be known through spiritual growth. They are not products of an intellectual process. They are products of the engaged, beating heart.

The Big Book is quite right in saying that our self-will and desire to control arise from a belief in our own absolute independence and a failure to recognize the connections we have, and need, to other people and to the larger world. The faith in our own capacity to function as solitary, self-propelling beings is both dangerous and inherently flawed. Isolation is a great limitation to mind, heart, and experience. But we may not, by the same token, wish to turn in dependence to a God of whom we cannot conceive or in whom we do not believe, as the Big Book suggests is our only option. Where does this leave us?

Part of what gives me a sense of balance in my spiritual life is a firm faith in the necessity of *interdependence* with the world in which I live. Giving and receiving, relying on and supporting. Letting go of ego, of the illusion of control, of the desire for certainty, allows me to be humble and aware of my own humanity, of my responsibility, and of other people. Paying careful attention both to what I need and to what I can offer up, I become a part of the human community.

And it is in that balance—between reaching deep into my spirit for what's wisest, most humble, and most vital in myself, and reaching out to offer what I have—that I find spiritual growth.

The upside of Step Three—Made a decision to turn our will and our lives over to the care of God *as we understood Him*—is that the Step explicitly says it is our own understanding of God that's required. The language does seem to assume a deity, a Him, of some kind, but if our understanding of spiritual sustenance is other than theistic, there is still room for us, and our beliefs, in this program.

The point of the Step, really, isn't God. There are people who would certainly argue with me on this point. But this is a program of action, and it is my belief that the point of this Step is *the act of turning it over*.

Some are quite comfortable with the idea that they turn their will and their lives over to the care and guidance of their Twelve Step group, or of the program itself; others can't quite conceptualize how that would work. I have found myself most comfortable with an understanding that the Step simply asks me to *let it go*. Not give it to a whom or a what. Just open my tight little fists and let it go.

Many of us have been holding on to our will and our lives with a vise grip, and have run them thoroughly into the ground. The decision we must make, then, is to loosen our hold on the things to which we cling. We need to let go, first, of the idea that we can run our lives by self-will, or—this is harder—that we can run them at all. The resistance and fear we often feel immediately upon hearing this should tell us something about how hard we try to control things and how hard this decision can actually be. The idea that we are masters of our lives, that our wills and egos and minds are enough to make them go according to plan, is an idea we dearly love, and one we will have no easy time letting go. We will let it go and take it back, let it go and grab for it again. The belief that we are in charge of how our lives proceed is delusional, yes, but it's a delusion we've been under for a very long time and one we hold because it makes us feel safe. Humans like few things more than a sense of safety, and we'll persuade ourselves of virtually anything in order to gain that sense of safety and immunity to the vicissitudes of life.

If we're not running our lives, though, who is?

This is the hard part, even for a nonbeliever, to swallow: nobody.

In theory, that's easy. Many of us can say that we are convinced that there is no power out there capable of or interested in running our lives. We are content to say there's no personified God, and cheerfully agree with ourselves and each other that an all-powerful, all-knowing God does not exist.

We are less cheerful when we have to face the fact that an all-powerful, all-knowing *self* does not exist, either.

But it is a fact we have to face. The illusion that we are in control of our lives can be disproven quite easily: take a look at your life as an addict. How did it go? How accurate was your belief that you were in charge?

Many people, certainly me, are convinced in early sobriety that once the addiction is "under control," their lives will come back under their control as well. I was pretty sure that once I stopped drinking, I would sail ahead most marvelously on my own steam and sense of purpose, nothing standing in my way. I would steer my little ship and there would never be rough waters and I would never run aground.

Wrong.

There's an old Irish saying I like: "Man makes plans, and God laughs." God or no God, our plans are not set in stone. Things will go as they go. It will not always be smooth, it will change course left and right, and it will not always be easy.

But it will be vastly easier if we do not fight. It will be infinitely less exhausting if we let go of the belief that things *must* or *should* go our way. It will be so much more peaceful—and I, for one, have been hoping for peace—if we just let it go.

During my first few years of sobriety, I fought Step Three kicking and screaming. I sat in my group on nights we discussed this Step and explained once again, to the very patient people there, that I was pretty sure that if I turned my will and my life over to God, he'd utterly screw it up. This was back when I was struggling to believe in a God at all and thought I really had to in order to be sober. The other members of my group listened, nodded, and then gently suggested that *I* had done a fairly good job of screwing my life up myself.

This was an excellent point; my life as an addict was a disaster. And honestly, my life in my first few years sober was a disaster as well, and I couldn't see why—I was doing everything right! Going to meetings, working the Steps, had a sponsor, did service work. And didn't for a minute believe I was not ultimately in control. I did not believe in God; I believed in my all-powerful, all-knowing self.

This faith in my own power ran my life aground as surely as drinking had. Eventually I had to do what I was being told to do: let the damn thing *go*.

The Steps are meant to be worked again and again, which is a good thing, because they only get a little below the surface of our hard outer shells the first time around. They are like any other spiritual practice; they take on new meaning each time we encounter them, and as time goes on, we can see and feel how different we've already become and are continuing to become. The Steps work us as much as we work them. This is another example of the way in which we do not control things, and must not try to. If we try to master the Steps intellectually—and I certainly made every attempt to do this in my first few years—we'll miss the point altogether, and we'll miss the chance to let them help us grow. Step Three is one of our first forays into our deeper spiritual selves, and if we do not take it on again and again, we will never tap into all the spiritual wisdom that we contain.

And we do contain spiritual wisdom, though we may never have seen it as such or may never have looked very hard. This Step teaches us to accept and to trust the world as it is, to accept people as they are, and to accept our lives as they will go. We are learning to accept that our concept of ourselves as solitary, self-run beings is flawed and that we are and must be more.

So what is that *more*? Who are we, and what do we believe? If no longer isolated by our perception that we are in control, and no longer hardened by our fear of letting go, what can we become?

These are questions that we have to ask as we begin to move beyond ourselves and out into the world.

❦

CHAPTER FOUR

Self-Knowledge

April

As we open both our hearts and minds and listen to the voice we can iden-
tify as spiritual in ourselves, we begin to recognize that there is much we
don't know about who we've become or who we want to be—a point of self-
estrangement we all reach at critical times in our lives. It is time to face the
work necessary to spiritual development by going within to explore who we
are and who and what we value in our lives and in this world—which we
lose sight of often and may lose sight of completely in addiction. The reason for
this self-examination is to reconnect us with the spiritual wisdom we contain
and, ultimately, to reconnect us with the world. We have come to Step Four.

There are few sounds on this isolated stretch of the Pacific coast—or rather, many sounds, but no human noise save that of my own blood beating in my ears. Through the open window comes the music of this place: The crash and roar of the ocean, gun-metal gray on this gray misty day. The chat and call of seabirds, and the scream of gulls. Occasional whispers of wind breathe through the tangle of trees and blackberry brambles and various vines that surround this small cottage, causing the threadbare white curtains to lift and fall like gesturing hands.

This cottage has two rooms, one bed. An old deadwood fence, the same gray as the sky, the wood softened with salt. Everything here is a little soft with salt and gives slightly to the touch. The salt wears away at things gently—the fences, the cottage, the firewood—and I am convinced the salt air sweeps up and over the sand dunes and into the little town, and there does its gentle work eroding the kite shop, the candy store, the shack of a used bookstore, and the towering shelves of crumbling, salt-eaten books.

This cottage has also two cups and two plates, and I have taken to setting out both, though I'm quite alone, when I make a meal. At Passover, the Jewish tradition is to set a place for the prophet Elijah, to show him that he's waited for. The centuries go by, and the people wait, living their lives around this space held sacred for their hope. Who knows what they wait for, exactly? The practice is not to know. The practice is to wait.

So I set out my other plate, just in case.

Spring comes to the coast a little later than it arrives inland. I flew into Portland and found myself in a flurry of blowing cherry and apple blossoms and the soft curved petals of magnolia flowers that tumble from the branches of the trees. The tulips, this year, have gone mad. The whole city's talking about it. There are tulips *everywhere*, enormous ones, so sleek and beautiful and many-colored they shock the eye, yards full of them, fields full of them, huge sweeps of color everywhere you turn. An old man I spoke to said he had planted 535 bulbs, and now had 535 flowers. "Every single one of them took!" he crowed. "Impossible, but true!"

When I was little, I used to lie on my stomach by the flowerbed in front of my house and peer down at the dirt. I pictured the bulbs under there, hard little knobs that I knew well could be used as weapons if thrown at, say, your brother, ugly little things that somehow contained a tulip or a daffodil or whatever that particular bulb held folded up tight under its skin. I tried to imagine how a tulip happened. Was it a caterpillar/butterfly sort of process? Did the caterpillar actually hold a butterfly in itself? When told these things, that tulips and butterflies and their ilk just sort of *transformed*, I was nonplussed. This was no kind of explanation. So I stared at the dirt, waiting for the tulip to emerge.

What a child knows about transformation is very little. What an adult knows, I think, is even less. Because a child at least remembers that transformation is *possible*. The child wants to know the mechanism by which it occurs, wants to know why it occurs and when, but at least the child is aware that it does take place. The child has evidence: She has her changing height marked in pencil on the wall. She knows that she herself is doing a tulip/butterfly sort of thing. She is a tiny scientist, and she has proof that the impossible occurs.

What do we lose as we grow older? Among other things, we lose wonder. We take the transformations of age as evidence of some nameless loss. We take the changes in our life, the comings and goings of things and people we love, as proof that life is pain. Not as proof that life is the very essence of change and transformation; that by its very definition, life shifts and seethes like the changing colors of the sea. We think life is static; we try to make it so; but the impossible occurs, and it transforms. And so do we.

I have come to the coast to celebrate two anniversaries: One, I am alive. My birthday is in a couple of days. And two, I am not dead. Neither seems probable at all; birth in itself is a pretty nifty process, and the miracle that addicts ever make it out of hell, and that I did, is one I wonder at all the time.

And here in my cottage I am waiting. These past few months, something has been stirring in me, waiting to be born. I am waiting to transform. My skin aches with it. Perhaps I am about to burst into bloom.

I step out onto the porch, feel the salt-mist gather on my face, and trudge through the shifting sand down to the water's edge. I take a walk I took a decade ago, when I arrived here, when here was a wall I hit hard.

I was sick with my addiction, nearly dead of body, spiritually empty, and with nothing left that I recognized as a self. The route I took to get to this little coast town was long and circuitous, and I drove it at 110 miles an hour, hell-bent on getting away from what remained of my life. This was where I stopped. This was where I finished off the last case of whiskey I had in my car. And this was where I looked up Alcoholics Anonymous (AA), called the number, and found my way to a meeting one town south.

I didn't get sober, not that try. But the people there kept me alive, literally, for a few weeks, and I remember their kindness well. It came as a shock: I had forgotten there was simple kindness to be found, and therefore to be given; I had forgotten I myself might contain it, or might contain any human goodness at all. I had forgotten what I ever knew of love. I had forgotten how to give. And having forgotten these things, I had stepped out of the human community and gone tumbling backward into a void.

Meeting after meeting, for the weeks I was there, these people fed me, made me drink juice, followed me home so they'd be sure I didn't drive off the road, and took me for walks. They'd talk. I'd listen. I knew none of them, really. They had no reason to care about me. The only reason was this, and it took me years to figure out: There is always reason to care. There is always reason to give. It is what we are here to do.

I remember one walk in particular. I was down by the water with a woman from the meetings. She was telling me her story; she'd gotten sober in jail. She was funny, and I think I startled myself by laughing. And then she stopped walking and turned to me. "You need to stop drinking," she said. "You're not going to be one of the lucky ones. You're going to die. Or kill someone with your car. And you won't do well in jail."

But I didn't think I could stop.

One of the Promises in the Big Book is this: "We will suddenly realize that God is doing for us what we could not do for ourselves" (page 84).

God. Or the world, the human community, time, tide. We transform each other; we transform within ourselves; we are transformed. It is a miracle that has no known source. It simply is.

We have proof. We are alive.

Today, I walk by the water until the sun starts to set. I sit down on a piece of driftwood the tide's carried high into the sand. It isn't strange, to me, that I've gone to an isolated place to be alone to celebrate another year gone by, another one ahead. I need to be by myself. There is work I need to do within, so I can do the next work I'm here to do in the world, whatever that turns out to be. Before I can do it, I need to look at where I've been, where I am, who I am, who I am not yet, and who I want to be.

I cannot bring the world anything if I do not know myself. Addiction taught me that. And addiction taught me that when I have questions like these, questions no one else can answer, I have to listen long and hard in stillness for the sound of my spiritual voice.

—

How well do we know ourselves? Here's a conundrum: for all the time we spend thinking about ourselves, our real knowledge of who we are is often quite limited. As the saying goes, "I'm nothing much, but I'm all I think about." What is it that we spend all this time thinking, when we think about ourselves? Does it really go to the heart of the people we are, to the ways that we operate in the world? And if we should want to know ourselves well, if we should want to look deeper, how would that be done?

We spend a great deal of time scuttling around on the surface of our lives, and on the surface of ourselves. We spend a great deal of time on the daily: what we want right now, what we need this minute, what is wrong with this situation, what is wrong with everyone else, what is wrong with us, and, conversely, why we are right. We put an extraordinary amount of effort into how we appear, or wish to appear, trying frantically to construct a sense of self out of how we are seen from without.

But who are we from within? What makes us who we are? If we stop for a moment and think, *Of what do I consist?* what is the answer we hear?

And many of us draw a blank. Because we cannot for the lives of us make out the sound of our spiritual voice.

Is the spirit who we ultimately are? Is there something we could call a "soul"? There are those who would argue that we are not more than scientific studies, a series of chemical interactions and responses that make us act certain ways, feel certain things. Personally, I think if that were the case, it would be rather remarkable in itself. But I don't actually think that's all we are. I think we are sentient beings who think and feel and are unique. Is that a soul? I think it matters very little what it is called. Because I think what many of us share is this: when we are ignoring it, that self or spirit or soul, that essence of who we are, we go hungry and feel a sense of emptiness and loss that we cannot escape until we are fed.

This emptiness draws many people to a God, and those people find their spiritual nourishment there. But there are those of us who do not feel a pull in that direction or find that same spiritual source when we search. I don't believe we can know who is "right," and I do not think it matters what answer we find. I think what matters is that we listen for the sound of the call.

Addiction shuts us off from the sound. That is not the only thing that silences the internal voice—but addiction does it quite well, and until we begin the work of listening hard, we will not know who we are, beyond creatures who crave.

As addicts, cut off from our spiritual selves, we lose sight of the need for self-awareness. We feel emptiness sharply but cannot stand to listen long enough to find out what it means, what we need, what it tells us about how we live. Instead we reach for the nearest thing at hand with which to fill it up. And so we go for years, not able to sit with the silence, not able to face what we have become—and becoming increasingly something we cannot stand.

And if we cannot stand ourselves—if we fear, and I think we do, that to even look at who we are would be too painful to bear—how do we live?

We don't, really. We survive. We get from day to day, propelled by fear, grabbing for what we think we need, and never truly knowing what would heal this spiritual void. We do not flourish, or grow, or become the people we have the potential to be. We lose our capacity to give or let anyone near, because we have closed ourselves off even from ourselves. Who can I be to you, if I am a stranger to me? How can I connect with you, if I am divorced from myself? If I cannot face the truth of who I am, how can I truly see you?

When we speak of self-knowledge, we are speaking of a knowledge that goes deeper than the ego, deeper than the simple identities we paste together from the scraps of our lives. We are not speaking of the self-absorption that consumes so much of our time; we are not speaking of how we are seen. We are more than these things. We have spiritual selves. But we cannot access those selves until we face what we fear.

We have been working toward a spirituality that is grounded in the here and now, that is based ultimately in action. The question we have been asking is, How do we live? We know how we lived as addicts. How do we live as people who are healing—healing within ourselves and moving outward to heal a wounded world?

It cannot be done until we know who we are.

The practice of self-knowledge—and it is a practice, ongoing, transforming, and never complete—is a form of spiritual action. Some of it is done in stillness; we begin to listen, an action that requires a certain measure of solitude. In its early moments, it's lonely. We are surrounded by the clutter of busy lives, lives busy in part because we clutter them up, trying to fill the nameless needs that we don't want to feel. When we step away from it, there's an awful initial sense of panic. The active practice of self-knowledge is not comfortable all the time, or easy. There's a reason we fear it. We know we aren't going to like all we find.

One thing we fear, curiously enough, is that we will find nothing at all.

The fact that we have been so long removed from our spiritual selves often gives us a sense not that we are spiritually hungry, but that we lack a self of any kind. We've lived on the surface a very long time, unwilling and often unable to look deeper, and gradually we do get the sense that we're empty. Not that we have a spiritual emptiness that needs healing, but that we have nothing within—that we *are* nothing at all.

The sense that we are only the sum of our parts—whatever we achieve, however we appear, whatever we own, however we try to prove ourselves—is not a good sense. It's an existential crisis: Do I even exist? If you take away the masks I wear, is there only blank space underneath?

We do not only wonder whether there is a void out there, in some great beyond. We fear there is a void within.

And if not a void, are we then only the sum of our wrongs?

This is what often triggers our knee-jerk reaction to the thought of self-examination: defense and denial. We know perfectly well what we've done; it eats away at us constantly, in the form of guilt, resentments, regrets. But we also justify. It's extremely hard to look at the past, and the addict's past is littered with the wreckage of people and lives, not only others', but our own. So we refuse to look.

But if we do not look at where we've been, we cannot honestly assess where we are. And if we do not know where we are, to state the obvious, we are *lost*. So how do we know where to go next? What gives us guidance? How do we know what to choose? How do we know what to do with our lives?

How do we live?

Action ultimately makes us who we are. We evidence ourselves by action. We are who we are not in theory, but in practice. And if we do not know who we are, we do not know what we do. We live, then, fumbling through our lives and swinging blind. The practice of self-examination is action we take on behalf not only of ourselves but of all those around us as well.

Self-knowledge is the foundation of a practical spirituality, a spirituality that ripples outward from the self into the world.

An honest assessment of oneself is inseparable from an honest assessment of one's life. We can't just take a look at who we think we are without seriously considering how we have lived—what we have done or not done, what we have said or left unsaid, choices we have made and choices we have refused to make. This is the only way for us to get an accurate picture of the people we were, the people we are, and the people we want to become.

The purpose of this assessment is not to make us feel one way or another about ourselves. Rather, the purpose is to know our hearts and minds, and it isn't idle knowledge. This is how we learn what we believe to be right. It is how we locate in ourselves the spiritual wisdom that tells us what our moral code should be. If guidance, for us, does not come in the form of a religious creed or the word of a God, then we must look to our moral and ethical standards about how we—not how everyone, but we—need to live.

In our lives as addicts, we have likely wandered from our own beliefs about the kind of people we need to be in this world. We have likely lost sight of what it is we want to do and how we want to live. An honest assessment of where we have been, where we are now, and where we want to go reopens the part of ourselves that contains our own ethical beliefs. When we have finally looked at what they are, we can begin to live by them again.

The practice of self-knowledge requires a degree of honesty we have not used in years, maybe never before. An attempt to do this without telling ourselves the truth or looking at the full scope of our lives is relatively useless. We've been running from the truth long enough. It also requires that we set down our pride. There's no seeing ourselves clearly through the smoke screen pride throws in our way. So we let go of ego as much as we can. We let go of the arrogant notion that we should have been perfect, and we let go of shame. We let go of judgment. The purpose of this, again, is not self-flagellation or self-congratulation. It's a search for accurate knowledge that can serve us as we move on.

So we begin with a look back at our lives. As addicts, many of us have gone careening back and forth from elaborate ruminating on the past to a flat-out refusal to acknowledge it at all. This is a different task. We look back and simply ask ourselves questions, and answer as honestly as we can.

Where have we been? What has our spiritual journey been like? Where did it take us? As we traveled, what choices did we make that affected our lives, the lives of others, our world? What is our story? Not only the story we tell others, and not the half-truths we've too long told ourselves. The true story of what brought us to the place where we now stand.

As we look back, our spiritual selves will stir. And in this process of examining the past, that stirring has something to teach us. We will feel grief. Regret. Happiness at certain memories, sorrow at some losses. We need to listen to those murmurings of the spiritual voice. It tells us where we have not lived as we wanted to live, and where we have been true to who we are. It shows us what we believe. The realization that we have not, by and large, lived according to those beliefs, is painful. But it helps us learn.

Our questions go on. Where did it begin? When did we start to turn a deaf ear to our spiritual selves and to feel the growing ache of spiritual emptiness at our core? How have we lived with that? How have we tried to fill it up? What gods have we been serving all this time?

What, in fact, have we done? What have our choices, our addictions, our emotions, our actions done to the people around us? How did that affect our behavior in the world, the things we did to others and ourselves? Action is not only evidence of who we are. It also *makes* us who we are. With each action, each choice, we shape ourselves and our lives. What have we made of ourselves? How have we moved our lives in the direction they've gone?

We are in great part the product of our own actions. So who have we become?

Where are we now? Where is this place we've arrived? We rarely look around and really take in the place we have created for ourselves. What are we doing here? How far have we strayed from the place we hoped to be—not that place of position or power we've longed for, but that place we once hoped would be our spiritual home? What world have we built for ourselves, and why? In this world, do our values hold? Are we living by what we believe? Or is this a world built in service of our fear?

Is it truly where we want to live? Is it a place where we can face ourselves? Or are all the mirrors cracked?

There is a basic human responsibility to determine how we want to build our lives—on what ethical foundations, based in what principled beliefs. When we live in addiction, we lose sight altogether of our own ethics, and our actions no longer fall in line with what we believe. As people who do not know an external Higher Power, though, we often wonder who's to say what's right, what's wrong, and how we should live. When we read in the Big Book that we must align our actions and our wills with God's will, we are quite at a loss as to what we should use as a basis of our choices and beliefs. Is it all arbitrary? Is there no moral standard after all?

If there were no ethics at work in the human community, we would not feel the pull to live a moral life, a life in which we believe. But we do feel that pull. Our spiritual voice may be quiet or so far buried that we can't hear it at all, but there remains in us a sense of right and wrong, and an awareness of when our actions do or do not fall in line with what we believe to be true. At this stage in our spiritual development, it's essential that we begin to bring our life in line with our sense of what is right. And that sense of right and wrong hinges entirely upon how we live in the world. Right and wrong cannot be determined by looking to oneself as an individual. Our sense of ethics must be determined by looking at ourselves as members of a larger community.

One way to interpret the idea of acting according to "God's will" when we do not believe in a God is this: We can act according to the world's need. We can make choices based on how our actions will impact the world. We can remember the butterfly effect. The ethical code we develop is one steeped in awareness that we are only one among many, that we contain moral wisdom, and that that wisdom needs to guide our lives and our paths through the world.

Where do we want to go? What do we want to do? Who do we want to become? Again, those questions are really two sides of the same coin; who we become depends on what we choose to do, the actions we take, the way we interact with the world. But how do we know, especially as we emerge from a time of spiritual crisis—the crisis of addiction, or any cycle of major spiritual transition in our lives—where we can go? Where we *should* go? What we can become, what we contain?

Walt Whitman wrote, "I contain multitudes," and all of us do. We are largely unfamiliar with all that we possess—flaws and gifts, capacities and limitations, spiritual wisdom, an ability to give and to love. The practice of self-knowledge acquaints us with the multitudes we contain, gives us access to the moral guidance we need, and provides insight into how we should choose. It is only by careful listening to the spiritual voice that we can know where our lives can go and who our spirits are trying to become.

We have to give our lives meaning. We have lived without it as addicts; we've replaced the search for meaning with the pursuit of something to satisfy our addiction's demands. This is a great part of the emptiness we've felt. A lack of meaning in our lives leaves us bereft of a reason to live each day. It is corrosive and eventually deadly. And so meaning must be found.

As we discover who we are as spiritual people, meaning emerges from all the places we have not been willing to look. There is no scope to meaning—it doesn't have to be grand. It is simply what matters to us at a deeper level than we've gone. In order to know what *we* mean, and what we want our *lives* to mean, we have to know how we have lived and who we are.

This is the purpose of the "searching and fearless moral inventory" of Step Four. It is not an exercise in self-abuse. It is not an indulgent wallowing in our history of wrongs. It is an investigation we undertake with equanimity and complete openness to whatever we find. Step Four helps us in our practice of learning to hear our own spiritual voice; and in that way, it leads us deeper into what we believe, what our spirits respond to, how they want to give and receive and grow. Step Four is a door we open onto meaning in our lives.

It didn't occur to me initially that Step Four was in any way a "spiritual Step" or that it could be worked in a spiritual way. Well, all the Steps can, and hopefully *will* be worked at a spiritual level. But upon my first examination of Four, it really did seem like—well, like an assignment for school. It seemed like there were rules and tidy formats and lists and ways of checking things off and being done.

There aren't. There is no right way to work Step Four, on paper at least; any way that works for you, anything that helps you get your thoughts down on the page, your resentments, your fears—and also your gifts and skills—will do the trick. What Step Four requires is a willingness to, as the Step itself says, be *fearless and thorough*. A partial examination of the parts of ourselves that feel safe to look at, a cursory glance over the decades of our lives—these are pretty much a waste of time. We are not assessing only who we are *now*. We're also looking at who we can become. And to answer that question, we have to look clearly at who we are not yet.

And so we go deeper, taking a stance of humility and open-mindedness, knowing we are only human, knowing we will not like all we find, and trusting also that the people we are and the lives that we live can be transformed through spiritual work.

We have spent some time during this cycle of spiritual renewal in dormancy, waiting, preparing for the evidence of our own transformation to slowly appear. Now, in this early springtime of the heart, we put into action what we have learned of trust, of acceptance, of letting go, and we begin to bloom.

CHAPTER FIVE

ᷰ

Reaching Out

May

There comes a point in our spiritual development when we are able to finally reach out and reenter the world as people who are no longer broken by addiction—or by any spiritual sickness—but are learning to be whole. At this moment in a spiritual life cycle, we may be better able to recognize in ourselves both the longing for participation in a broader human community and the need to bring our full, flawed, spiritual selves—honestly and without reservation, fearlessly and without shame or regret—with us as we go. We have come to Step Five.

It began with letters.

The first letter came in a small envelope, on yellow notebook paper, written in a forward-slanting scrawl. The letter sat on my desk unopened for a while. I worked in the circle of light cast by a small lamp, the letter at my right hand. I glanced at it from time to time, set down my pen, turned it over once or twice, as if it were an object I'd never seen before, some kind of strange thing unearthed in an archeological dig.

One night I opened the letter, unfolded it, and began to read.

The place where I lived was mostly empty, save for the enormous desk, an equally enormous magenta couch, a small table in the kitchen, one chair, and a single mattress on the floor. The walls were bare. The evidence of one failed attempt at keeping a plant sat on the windowsill, cracked brown leaves dangling out of the pot.

I don't remember now when I'd last talked. I must have, of course. There must have been people whose lives brushed up against mine in passing, as I took the bus or went to the store or opened the multiple locks to my apartment door, people who lived across the hall, the postman who brought the mail. But now, many years later, I remember the time as silent. Silence in my small rooms, silence occupying space in my mouth. The clicking off of the lamp, the sounds of nocturnal people as I leaned my forehead on the window in the dark and looked down at the street below.

I'd been moving about this tiny world in silence for quite a while when I finally opened the letter that sat on the desk.

Come to the desert, it said. *It's spring.*

Before the apartment, I'd been living in what I knew of hell. The apartment was a kind of quiet heaven. In the apartment, I was no longer drunk. I was no longer a tornado ripping through people's lives. I was no longer careening through my days in terror, racing toward something or away from something, I couldn't say which. I was no longer lying on my friend's floor holding a beer and crying that something was wrong and I didn't know what.

Now I knew what. Now I lived in a place without the thing that had been killing my body and destroying my mind and, though I wouldn't have known how to say this at the time, the thing that had been drowning my spirit as well. Now the cupboards and freezer and fridge were empty of booze.

But I was full of a silence I didn't know how to break.

I sat with the letter a long time, reading it over, turning the pages again and again.

The house is made of stone and light, the letter said. *Spring in the desert is something to see.*

I took out a notebook and scribbled. *I don't know you,* I said. *You don't know me.*

So tell me, came the reply.

I sat there with that letter and thought, *I can't.*

I began to look for the letters in my mailbox. They came steadily. They told me stories, described the desert, described the desert town where this faceless friend lived. I pinned them to the blank wall above my desk. I looked at them as I worked, and then, when I'd run out of things to work on, when I couldn't avoid it any longer, when I was bursting with what could be said, what I wanted to say, I wrote back.

I wrote in theories and abstractions. I sent ideas and flurries of words. I told no stories. But I also told no lies.

Then the photo came. It showed the house of stone and light.

I sent a photo of my dead plant.

The photo of sunrise over red mesas came.

I sent a photo of my friend's letters pinned all over my wall.

The photo of the river of melted mountain snow sluicing down a crevice in the dry sandy rock.

The first day over 100, the next letter said. *Hurry. Soon the hummingbirds will come to the canyons.*

I packed up my car, got rid of the desk and magenta couch and single bed, and hit I-35 heading south.

The desert, in May, is arid and hot. It's called foresummer drought. The streambeds have gone mostly dry. But drought does not tell the whole story. The story of the desert in May is told at night.

The desert is noisy. There is a clicking, hissing, rushing sound when you walk it—furious winds rush down from the mountains and cut across wide bare places, twisting the road signs on old abandoned highways into spirals. The tiny, profuse wildflowers that cover the hills and desert floor with color in April have been replaced by the striated colors of high rocks packed down over millions of years, the dun and green seascape of cacti and sagebrush, the swaths of sand that waver in the rising heat.

But the desert in May is mostly nocturnal, and it's at night that you imagine you can hear (or maybe you really can hear) the roar of the billion-year-old ocean that once covered this ground. They find the fossils of sea-horses here, and shells. Things buried under layer after layer of volcanic rock and hard-packed sand.

And it's at night that the cacti bloom. Saguaro, senitas, organ pipes, and the night-blooming cereus, whose white flowers open under moonlight and close before dawn. The ironwood and smoke trees loosen their laven-der blossoms. And there are all manner of red trumpet-shaped flowers that open to welcome the hummingbirds who come to the canyons, just as my friend said they would.

At night I spoke. Haltingly at first, then in quick rushes, and then fell silent again. My friend and I sat at the table in the cool stone kitchen with a small light between us. He told me stories. He was an old man, full of quiet laughter, and had lived alone a long time. But his solitude had not been lonely, or silent, had not been words and secrets swallowed. His had been the rushing, clicking, hissing story of the desert moving through its seasons as he moved through the seasons of a joyful life.

By speaking, he taught me to speak. By telling the truth, he taught me that I could tell the truth as well. By listening, he bore witness to my life in a way I had never borne witness to anyone else's or my own. In that, he taught me to listen and taught me the value of bearing witness to the emergence of another person into themselves and into the world.

We sat at the table. Through the windows, the desert ocean whispered under the louder sound of cicadas and rustling long-nosed nectar-feeding bats and singing red-spotted toads. Night bled into day bled into night as secrets came out into the little light, lost their poison, became simply the facts of a life. Choking regrets became griefs that could heal. Corrosive shame, when set on the table between us, lost its power and was let go.

We said goodnight, went to our cool stone rooms, his with his easel, mine with a table and chair. I fell asleep looking at the cactus that grew just outside my window, watching the night cereus bloom.

―

For years, we walked along, dragging the dusty bag of our pasts behind us, carrying in our wake every secret, every sorrow, every shame. We carried our wrongs, never allowing them into the light of day where we could see what we'd done and so keep from doing it again. We carried our regrets, our resentments, the recriminations we nursed toward others and ourselves. What we did not love in ourselves, we stuffed in the bag. What we hated in our lives went into the bag as well. Our fears and our failures. All we wished we had not done, all we wished that we had. All we swore we'd carry with us to our grave.

It's a burden more than we humans can bear. I could not bear it. I tried to set it down and walk away more times than I can count. I tried every time I drank to feel something else, to be someone else. But morning always came, white and piercing, and secrets I'd swallowed still poisoned me, and the bag that I carried was still by the bed.

The longing to be someone else, to re-create oneself, is a relatively common human wish. We want desperately to escape what has happened, what we've done, and who we have been. We try every trick in the book. We lie. We deflect. We omit. And we perform. We are masters of theater, always ready with a new costume and a new mask that will make us, for once, who we think we ought to be.

And we do it for such simple reasons: We want to be respected, and we want to be loved. And we believe that we, as we are, do not justify either respect or love.

We so often believe that in order to be loved, we must be perfect. Better than human. Not flawed. It's a form of arrogance, really. My notion that I could ever *be* perfect, and gain the love and respect I so craved for that perfection, was predicated on a faith in my own superhuman self. I believed that if I just tried a little harder, I could shake off the demons that tapped at my shoulder; if I talked a little louder, I could drown out the sound of my whispering secrets; if I ran a little faster, I'd be a blur, and then no one could see the ragtag mess I was.

It was all right with me, then, that in order to be loved for someone I was not, I could never be truly loved, because I could never be truly known. I accepted that, because I was quite certain that if I *were* known, if I allowed anyone close enough to me to see me, they'd walk away, and even that shadow of love I'd hoped for would be gone.

It never occurred to me that I could lay down the burden of all I carried with me—the shame, the self-hatred, the secrets, the regret—and learn not only to be loved, but to love.

How could I possibly love someone else when I couldn't begin to conceive of showing them who I was? How could I see who *they* were? How could I close the gap I created between myself and everyone I met?

And until I learned to love, how would I heal?

This stage in the life of the spirit is not one we can avoid, nor should we. If we stop here, we cut ourselves off from the healing that comes of loving and learning to love. This is the time in our lives when we lay down the mask, lay down the burden we've carried, and go out into the world unguarded and undisguised. As we are. Flawed. Human. Raw and broken in places. And beginning to heal.

Nearly everyone I've ever encountered in sobriety has faced this stage of spiritual development with fear that ran the gamut from trepidation to full-blown terror. It's taught me something about just how much I myself fear being real—imperfect, vulnerable—and how much a frightened part of me fears being "found out." How many of us have felt like frauds? Felt certain that if we were really known, if someone else knew the "truth" about us, their love or respect for us would go up in smoke?

And so we dance faster, trying to be what we think they want, trying not to be ourselves. This is a dance we do entirely alone.

But we have come to a different place, lately. The time we've spent dormant, the time we've spent learning to listen for the spiritual voice, the time we've put into a growing knowledge of self, has brought us to this place where we are aware of our fear of others, our fear of their judgment, our fear we will not be loved. The self-delusion that allowed us to live double lives for so long has begun to break down. The people we truly are have begun to show through. And we are aware of a new spiritual hunger: we long to be a part of the human community again. And we are ready to enter it *as we are*. As our simple, full, flawed selves.

Because at last we have realized this much: Not only will we receive something from that human community. Finally, we see that we have something to give.

⁓

Behind the practice of sharing your story, your truth, with another person—and facing it clearly yourself—is not a lesson in humiliation, as we often fear it will be. Instead, the practice of truth-telling and bearing witness to another's truth is about humility and opening up. As we let go of our secrets and put an end to our lies, we break down the seemingly impenetrable barrier that we have held between ourselves and other people for so long. We open a channel between our spirits and theirs, and enter into spiritual connection with them at last.

And this is how we enter the human race again: as real people, spiritually alive, spiritually open, and spiritually connected to others. Grounded in the humility of honest self-awareness, we become aware of others in a way we never have been before. This is what the Big Book means when it says we go beyond spiritual experience and begin to have a spiritual *existence.* This is where we begin to live as spiritual creatures here, now, in this world.

We cannot move into this stage while we still cling to all the things that hold us back. Those things are familiar and comforting; they are the source of pain we're used to, rather than the source of the peace we're ready to enter now. When I came into sobriety, I quickly discovered that the idea of spiritual peace was nearly as frightening as the idea of staying spiritually sick—because it was wholly unfamiliar. And I found myself clinging with a death grip to things it was long past time to let go. I clung to my anger, for fear that without it I'd lose some mysterious (imaginary) "edge." I clung to my resentments, because I had been nursing them so long I couldn't imagine life without their poisonous satisfaction. I clung to my regrets, and they were legion, going over and over the smallest mistakes I'd made as well as the biggest, hating myself for all I'd done and all I'd failed to do.

My father, a wise fellow, told me this Celtic prayer the other day: *What's done is done; what's been left undone has been left undone. Let it be.*

This stage of our spiritual lives brings us to a level of acceptance that we have not reached before now. At some point, we all must come to grips with where we've been, what we've done, and what we have yet to do. That *coming to grips* is not about self-flagellation. It is not about putting on a crown of thorns. It is about looking squarely at ourselves, our characters as they have evolved thus far, and our lives as we have lived them up to this moment. The purpose is not to wallow in self-recrimination and regret. The purpose is to learn perhaps our hardest lesson: that of accepting who we are.

That we are only human comes as something of a shock to many of us.

That we can only *be* human, no matter what we do, is a hard thing to face; many of us have held very dear the notion that if we tried hard enough, we could be, or could at least appear, superhuman. Perfect. Unassailably good. Without blemish or flaw. This standard to which we have held ourselves has had a very curious, rather contorted effect: we have simultaneously lost all respect for ourselves, judged ourselves lacking, and felt like the most regrettable specimens of humanity around; and, afraid of feeling yet worse, we have also resisted looking very hard—or at all—at ways in which we have, in fact, screwed up.

But our time in self-examination has allowed us, finally, to take that long hard look. Now comes the next step: we speak.

At this point, many of us are tempted to ask why. *Why on earth should we open those old wounds?* we ask, as if we do not scratch them open ourselves all the time. Why should we tell someone else about all these things only we need to know? Whose business is it, really, but our own?

What we mean is, What will they think of me? Will they respect me? Will they forgive me? Am I allowed to have failed? Or does that cost me my place in the human race?

We have been influenced perhaps more than we would like to think by religions in which we claim not to believe. Our notion of *sin* is very strong, as is our notion that our sins—our wrongs, our mistakes—are enough to cut us loose from human love and companionship. But humans do make mistakes, do wrong one another and themselves. And those of us who do not connect with or believe in a God find ourselves asking this: How can I be forgiven?

Predicated on the notion of sin and forgiveness, our ideas about human wrong and restitution linger in a religious context in which we find no comfort and in which we have no faith. For this reason, we need to reconceive for ourselves what we mean when we acknowledge that we have done harm; we need to find a source of reassurance that our mistake does not cut us off from human companionship and love—that our human error has not shut us out of the human race.

If we sense there is no divine source of forgiveness, we often wonder to whom we can turn for comfort and guidance when we have done harm. We may feel adrift in a moral conundrum, uncertain what is sin, what is right, what can be forgiven, what can be saved. What I have realized after many long nights awake with my wrongs is that I have to reframe the question. The question is not really *Who will forgive me?* but *How can I change?*

And that is part of the reason we bring our stories out into the open, so that we can see them clearly and so that they can be seen by another person. We are not seeking forgiveness by some external force; we are seeking truth and clarity in how we move ahead in our lives. That truth provides us with the guidance we require as we look over the things we've done and the people we've been. It provides us with the map for how we can take action from now on.

Perhaps it is not the kind of comfort provided by some religions—a personal comfort, given by a personified figure, who tells us that we are forgiven and are saved. But it is an enormous comfort to feel as if we have transformed from an old self into a new one, a stronger and truer one, who is better able to live in an ethical and moral way. We seek that spiritual comfort through our own action, rather than hope that comfort will come from a source outside ourselves.

Telling our stories, in their entirety, is one of the actions we take in the search for spiritual peace. Its closest corollary in religious tradition is, of course, confession. Many of us perhaps look too much askance at the practice of confession; we often associate it with religious judgment, punishment, and an angry God. But confession, at least in some traditions, is intended not as a shameful exposure of secrets held but as a release of what we hold that poisons us, or breaks our hearts when held alone. When we finally open our mouths to speak, it isn't so that we can confess and be judged. It is so we can release what weighs us down, and be healed.

One aspect of religious confession that can be instructive here is this: part of the purpose of confession, beyond lifting the burden of the confessor, is to allow that person to more rightly align with God's will. A very similar thing is at work in our efforts to tell our whole truth, to face it ourselves and to bring it to another person. We may not be in the business of trying to line up with God's will. But we do want—we need, really—to bring ourselves into right relation with the world in which we live. The harm we have done to others reflected our departure from the needs of that world and the people in it; the harm we have done to ourselves has damaged our ability to bring good into the lives of those around us and the larger world. As we bring our stories into the light of day, we are able to clearly see why we wandered from what we know and believe to be right, from what we believe of ourselves and the way we want to live.

And as we speak, we find the guidance we need in the spiritual connection that opens between ourselves and the person who listens. We find wisdom present in our own spiritual selves, and we find acceptance as our listener does not turn away. Simultaneously, the path we seek toward new action becomes clear. We need only listen closely to others and to our own spiritual voice as we finally let it speak.

—

The transformation from spiritual sickness to spiritual growth is a transition that requires us addicts to work Step Five. This Step puts an end to the isolation we've both sought out and suffered through, the alienation from the world that we have unnecessarily brought on ourselves. The silence and loneliness of secrets, shame, and lies create a state of existential despair; from this place of absolute isolation, we are unable to reach out. We are also unable to face ourselves. We spend our time hiding our face from the world and refusing to look in the mirror.

When I was in the heart of my addiction, I could not be alone with myself. The sound of all I wasn't saying made an unbearable roar in my head, and the only thing that tuned it out was alcohol; gradually, even that didn't do a very good job. But I couldn't be with anyone else, either—I felt like I was choking on my secrets, afraid at every moment they'd find out what a fraud I really was, what a failure, what a waste. And so I spent my days in increasing isolation and in increasing silence, more and more poisoned by all the things I refused to say. I lay in bed drinking, literally sick with scotch and shame.

Had I known then that all that would be required of me to find some measure of spiritual comfort would be to *speak*—and put down the scotch—I might have done it sooner. Hard to say. At that time, the concept of telling someone else, or even admitting to myself, the person I believed myself to be, was beyond frightening. It was an impossibility. I felt certain I would be struck dead by a God in which I didn't believe.

Which is to say, I felt certain I would lose whatever love I had left.

When I finally came clean, though—when I finally listened for and then spoke up with a spiritually alive voice—I found I was nothing special. It was a mind-boggling relief. I wasn't so awful. I wasn't required to be great. I was simply a human like any other, a pastiche of assets and flaws.

Spirituality based in an honest assessment of self is a humble spirituality. I'm not sure there's any other kind.

Step Five puts into action the humility we began to gain during our work of self-knowledge in Step Four. And when we put humility into action, we finally reenter the human race. No longer tangled in our own self-hating pride, no longer swallowing secrets we should not keep, no longer isolated by our own fear—when we find the spiritual peace of humility within ourselves, we find our way to the humanity of which we've longed to be a part.

Without humility, we cannot fully connect with other people. Step Five brings us out of isolation and into relationships we need for reasons we may not have been aware of prior to sobriety. When I was in active addiction, I saw relationships primarily as a condition of vulnerability that I couldn't tolerate. I was not aware of such things as fearlessly loving, fearlessly being present, giving without expectation of return. But those things are the stuff of spiritual life and spiritual growth. Without relationships, without others, we are spiritually adrift, and we do not learn to move beyond our own selves, our own needs, and our own fears.

I have often heard people say that spiritual sickness and addiction are the product of a "God-sized hole" within the self. But in my own life, the great emptiness I have felt, the echoing sense of nothing within, was filled when I began to connect with other people. Spiritual life cannot be a state of continuous solitude. We cannot find spiritual fullness without learning to give and receive. When we mistrust others, when we lock ourselves away out of pride and fear, we shut ourselves off from the wisdom and love that other people give us, and teach us to give.

Step Five requires a bravery of a kind we do not often recognize. It is rare that we think of being ourselves—simply ourselves, nothing more—as brave. But we are. We have spent so much time hiding behind secrets and carefully constructed alternate selves that we often don't even know who we are underneath. The work of self-examination that we did in Step Four prepared us to be honest about who we are, even as it seems frightening when we begin. We are ready for this. And it's time. Until we begin the work of moving beyond our past and the people we were, we will remain trapped, and we will not grow.

The seasons of spiritual fullness and reaching out will come in cycles in our lives. We will go dormant again, and learn to listen in new ways, and have new things to bring out into the world when we return. A snake sheds its skin again and again. It grows within this skin, and then grows beyond it. Then it rubs its nose against a rock, and breaks through, and leaves what it no longer needs behind.

CHAPTER SIX

The Moral Self

Early Summer (June and July)

A moment of spiritual lushness and vitality comes as we become more aware of both our spirits and the spiritual lives and needs of others. In this moment, we are prepared to examine, perhaps for the first time, perhaps simply anew, what the word moral *means to us. If we are to live meaningful and interconnected lives in this world, we face critical questions about who we feel we need to be and how we need to live—no longer only for ourselves, but immersed in and answerable to the world. Prepared by months of work within the self and a nascent beginning of connection, we are ready to let go of all that has held us back from being our full moral selves. We have come to Steps Six and Seven.*

I decide to walk. There's a path that runs 277 miles along the northwestern curve of Lake Superior, into and out of the Sawtooth Mountains, through boreal forests, over thirteen rivers and a bounty of creeks and streams. I know the path pretty well. I've hiked my way along sections of it, returning to explore longer stretches as time went on. But I've been away a few years, and this year I get it into my head that I'm going to walk the whole thing.

So I find myself back in my car, heading north. City gives way to prairie grasses and farmland. The elevation begins to climb as you enter the foothills of the mountain range. And then you turn a corner of the highway, and the massive, glittering blue body of the lake is flung out below you, reaching to the horizon and the edge of what the eye can see.

Rocky cliffs rise up along the road. The twisted ropes of water that were frozen in January come flooding down, and up ahead you can see the first of dozens of waterfalls that send a sound of rushing, whispering water out into the forests. I park, gather my things, and set out on the path, listening to the sound of wild water filling the air.

The path is wide at first, well traveled at the mouth of the trail, and then it narrows to a less-worn, overgrown ramble through underbrush and trees, over tangled roots and rocks. Summer has come to the forest. There are a thousand shades of green, from the nearly black pines to the manifold colors of aspen, ash, and silver birch, to the thick-leaved growth that covers the forest floor. At my feet, crowding the rough path, the fragile wild-flowers of spring have given way to the bursting oranges and purples and reds of starflowers, Indian pipe, and devil's paintbrush. Everywhere around me, the forest is sharp with the smell of hot sun on growing things.

My feet move me through the forest, over the uneven ground, along the cliffs high above cascading rivers, into broad high-grass meadows flooded with pale white light. As I walk, I feel myself set down what I was carrying—whatever it was, whatever its nature and name—and move forward, my body lighter, my spirit beginning to breathe.

I've traveled this path as a child in autumn, spellbound and silent as I ran through the brilliant colors the forest turns before it fades, pausing to turn and call back to those who followed me too slow. I raced down this path as if it were years, and soon I was walking it as a young woman, hiking hard into the high reaches I'd never seen before, scrambling over rough patches, standing at the very edge of the cliffs that cut away and fell hundreds of feet into jagged whitewater, feeling a vertigo from which I could not pull away. I've stumbled upon black bears and big cats and held very still, heart pounding with the rush and fear of things vastly larger than me.

I've walked with people I loved. Some of those people are lost now, to the passage of time and life's ending, and some are lost only to me, through my own mistakes and unkindness. Those who followed my small racing self as a child are too old now to walk these cliffs and paths, and though they are not here, for them I walk slow. Those at whom I lashed out and left as a young woman are somewhere on the map, but I don't know where, and for them I walk with a care and gentleness I lacked then.

As I walked—and say it *was* years I walked through—I gathered much I needed, and much I did not need, and much I needed then but no longer do and am ready to lay down.

So I walk this time alone, in the fullness of high summer, in a kind of peace that has come in the middle years of my life. It is the peace of the end of addiction and chaos and breathtaking pain. And it is the peace of knowing there is no race to the end of the path. There is no end, in fact, to the path. The forest is ever-changing, coming alive and in the same moment dying, new fiddlehead ferns unfurling in the dark hollows of the mossy felled logs over which I climb.

This is the place to which I return, knowing myself more clearly than I ever have, and not yet as clearly as I one day will. This is where I come to let that which is finished for me die, and to find what is new and unknown. When I turn to look back at the years I've come through, at what I have done, what I have not done, who I eventually became, it is not an easy view. It is a view of the gradual closing of my spirit like a door, a view of all I littered in my fearful, raging wake. I do not like to look at it. But I have to, if I am going to allow my spirit to open further. When I allow that opening, I step into this interconnected world as the person I want to be. I step into this place, this moment in time, and I begin to fully live.

This is the fullest season of the spirit, when we find in ourselves the abandon and lushness of summer, a season of spiritual growth. It is this abandon that makes us willing. It is this fullness that opens us to letting go, opens our tightly clenched hands and lets fall all that we do not need to hold, all that we no longer need to be. This is the summer of the spirit—the smell of sun, the rushing sound and spray of wild water set free from the ice.

After a hard climb up the narrow bank of a wide, fast-moving river, I reach a plateau in the mountain's side. I'm at Devil's Kettle Falls. A massive waterfall tumbles down into a shallow pool at my feet, and from that pool it rushes down into another falls, and another after that, all the way down to the Great Lake. But the pool where the water pauses here is clean and clear to the bottom, and takes its time ambling over and around wet green and gray and black rocks. The afternoon sun touches the rippling water in flashes of silver and white.

I stand on the bank awhile. Then I walk in. I balance my way over the slippery stones, make my way to the center of the pool, and sit down, clothes and all. I wrap my arms around my knees and look out over the falling river, through the broad opening of trees that allows it to pass through. I can see for miles, down the mountains and foothills, all the way out to Lake Superior, its silver expanse stretching on and on.

I sit there a long time, clean water rushing around my body. Then, as the sun begins to turn the sky over the horizon a hazy rose, I get up, walk back to the bank, step back onto the path, and walk on.

—

We've been walking toward this. The spiritual moment at which we have arrived is one we've been approaching for a while—truly, since we were broken open by addiction, or whatever source of pain caused us to hear the echo of the spiritual emptiness we felt. That breaking-open, as painful as it was, was a gift. It led us to look honestly at the barren places in our hearts, the closed places in our minds, the secrets we held that were poisoning us. The breaking-open caused us to look at ourselves in a way we had not looked in a long time, if we ever had looked with honesty at all.

In the moment of that breakage, when we admitted our powerlessness over addiction, or faced the reality of whatever pain we were in, we heard the cry of our spirits. And we began to walk.

Here we arrive at a clearing. This is a space of spiritual simplicity, a place of spiritual clarity. From here we see where we have been, and where we are, and where we hope to go. In this place, the work we need to do is not complex. But it's not easy, either, and it's not painless. We have come here to transform, and we transform by letting go.

There are things we have carried into this clearing that we have walked with too long, and as we let them down, one by one, we'll feel the lightness that comes when we do not carry a burden of spiritual pain. That spiritual pain we have felt comes in great part from ways we have done harm—to others, to ourselves. The pain comes from living at war with the world. It comes from holding on to beliefs and values that serve addiction, or anger, or ego, or fear, and do not serve others, and do not serve our spiritual selves. It comes from our growing alienation from the moral core that once allowed us to live in peaceful relationships, and at peace in ourselves.

That moral core—the moral self—is no different from the spiritual self. It is the spiritual self at work in the world. We have walked through spiritual seasons that required us to be alone, to restore, to prepare. Now we are at the moment where we need to consider ourselves as full members of humanity, responsible and answerable to the human community. We are no longer living as addicts, operating under a solitary morality of isolation, self-destruction, and fear. The morality we're reaching now—perhaps for the first time, perhaps simply anew—is one that calls us to be aware of our spiritual values and beliefs about how we should live, and at the same time remain ever conscious of the spiritual lives and needs of others.

It is this moral interconnectedness that will open the door to the world that has seemed closed to us for so long. This moral strength allows us to reach beyond ourselves, beyond our own wants, beyond our own perceptions, and touch the life of someone else. This is spiritual action in the world, and it is what brings so much meaning to our human experience.

And until we make the choice to heal our moral core, we cannot begin.

How is that healing done? Many of us look inward and think we see a moral core rotted beyond recognition; we despair of ever becoming morally whole and healthy again. But we will. Look at where we are. Look back at the road we've walked. That we are alive is astonishing; that we are *spiritually* alive more astonishing still. There exists in us a moral core that has not rotted, died, or dissolved. It's simply been crushed and hidden by all the other things we've gathered up because we thought we needed them, or things we did need at one time that have since become toxic to us in our movement toward spiritual health. The moral core is there. It's looking a little peaked, true. It needs some care and feeding. But it will heal, and thrive, and show us how we need to live.

That is the spirituality of life here on the ground: How do I live? Without a vital, thriving moral sense, we do not know the answer. That's the work we're here to do now. We've been prepared by all that we've done so far on this spiritual search. We've developed the willingness, honesty, and humility that we need. So we begin.

In the Twelve Step literature, the Steps where we encounter a specific need to develop moral integrity—Six and Seven—would have us do so by asking a Higher Power to remove our character defects. For the nonbeliever, this poses obvious questions: In the absence of such a power, who, precisely, do we ask to take care of this for us? And if there is no one to ask, what do we make of the idea that our moral failings will be "lifted" from us and that we will be "granted" release from the moral traps we have built and in which we live? How do we deal with the passive-voice language that assumes the clear and present existence of an outer force that has the power and desire to grant this release? And if we do not believe in such a force, will our defects of character be taken from us after all?

We need to return here to the issue of transformation—our capacity for it, its potential within us, the simple fact that transformation in human life, in the human spirit, occurs. Whether one believes that transformation is effected by the will of an outer force, or the willingness of an inner self, does not change the reality of transformation as a phenomenon of spiritual experience. All we need to know is that it does occur. We have proof of that; we have our living, breathing, ever-expanding spiritual selves.

It is this spiritual capacity for transformation, which we have already begun, that tells us *yes*—our moral struggles will lessen and we will feel greater moral clarity as we work toward change and as we allow change to take place within us. It will not take place all at once, or only once. It is a lifelong evolution of the spiritual, moral self.

And it is willingness, not will, that sparks this evolution in us. It is not will that moves us forward, any more than it was will that began to open our spirits. This entire journey has been a matter of allowing ourselves to expand spiritually—not to force our spirits to speak but to *let* them do so, not to power our way through spiritual struggle but to open to its wisdom, not to chase spiritual wholeness but to let it arrive in its own time. This is the paradox of *being transformed,* not by an outer force but by inner spiritual forces working in accordance with the world.

So we ask again: Will our moral defects be lifted? Perhaps it's better if we are aware of the role we play ourselves in this process of moral change. Perhaps it's clearer when we recognize our own need to—not for the first time—*let those defects go*. We have tapped into a bottomless well of spiritual strength. The task we encounter again is the need to use that strength to take the spiritual action of letting go.

This is the same way that our addiction itself was lifted: when we recognized our human limitations and spiritual brokenness—when we let go of all that had held us back—our addiction did lift from our shoulders. The lock on our spirits was sprung, and we began to come back to life. The release we find from addiction is a release we can find from our moral and personal struggles as well. We can leave the traps in which we sit and lay aside the things we have gathered that weigh us down. This release is a spiritual release. By letting go what hinders us, we set ourselves free.

And in that setting free of our spirits lies our unhindered capacity to be spiritually engaged with and working in the world.

We have already discovered plenty of things in our selves in need of change, plenty of moral and personal defects that keep our spirits locked away from even ourselves and of little use in the world. But there is a reason we have held on to these things so tightly and have such a difficult time letting them go. Since I've begun the process of chipping away at my character defects and trying to restore strength to my moral center, I have often felt that there was a small, hard, mean self blocking the way of a more peaceful, grateful, spiritually alive self, one that is capable of giving, capable of connection with others and with the world. The small, mean self I sense is the part of me that clings to my character defects with the vise grip of a child, desperate not to let them go, terrified of what will happen if I do. This is the self blindly driven by ego and fear. And this is the addict who lives in me still.

The devolved, collapsing moral structure of that frightened addict will continue to undergo repair for my entire life. I believe it is imperative for all of us, addicts or not, to engage in moral growth for a lifetime. But my job is not to tell anyone else what his or her moral structure should be. My only job—and it's plenty—is to let go of the morally questionable, damaging, selfish, or otherwise harmful values I have come to hold , and replace them with values that have spiritual meaning and worth.

We gather up damaging values over time, and we hold on to them for a reason. At one time or another, these values served us. That they no longer do is a hard fact to absorb. When we have been damaged ourselves, we develop a moral structure of self-preservation. When we have been left, we leave. When we have been raged at, we rage. When we have been used, we use others. When we have been through pain—any degree of it—we will go to insane lengths to avoid feeling pain ever again, and we live in fear of feeling at all.

And then our addiction caves in on our heads, and we have to begin again.

What served us in our earlier lives has turned on us now, and on those we loved as well, and limited our usefulness to the world. We are at the point where we must redefine every value we thought we held. What do we reply, when we truly ask ourselves, What holds meaning? What holds value in this world? What do I want my life to mean? The answers we give often fly straight in the face of what we have done and how we have actually lived.

I've heard "character defects" defined as "that which interferes with our usefulness to the world." Addiction is one of the things that can divorce us from the world and its need, rendering us useless to others, taking away our capacity to give, and preventing us from receiving spiritual connection as well. We need to let go of those values that served our addiction and find in ourselves the values that serve others and that nourish our spiritual selves.

The values that serve addiction are the very ones that shut down our spirits. Even those that do not bring immediate pain to us—those that are easy to identify and that we want to be rid of anyway—may still close us off from spiritual life. So much that feeds the ego feeds addiction—resentment, judgment, envy, self-righteous pride—and starves the soul, denying our spirits the connections they crave in the form of forgiveness, respect, and love.

The moral structure we gradually build within ourselves when we live by values that serve only our pain and our fear leaves no room for spiritual growth at all. We do become small and mean, closed and withholding and angry, self-annihilating and self-absorbed. And because our actions arise from our moral structure—however flawed that structure may be—we act not from a place of spiritual and moral evolution, but from a place of instinctual, animal fear.

The book *Twelve Steps and Twelve Traditions* says, "The chief activator of our defects has been self-centered fear—primarily fear that we would lose something we already possessed or would fail to get something we demanded" (page 76). So we have to look at what it is we demand. We have to look at what we think we want. Because the demands we place on others and on the world, the infinite wants and dissatisfactions with which we entertain ourselves, reflect a value that we cannot afford to keep: the value of *having*.

We need—our spirits are desperate for—the value of *giving*. Only when we have dislodged the deeply embedded desire to have, to keep, to own, will we make room for the spiritual self, which longs to give. It is in giving that the spirit connects with and works in the world. Until we allow it to do that, we will remain disconnected, isolated, and deeply afraid. Our lives as moral, spiritual beings will not begin until we value giving more than we value what we have. If our question truly is, *How do I live?* then our answer can only be *I give*.

What have we sought? What have we chased? What have we held sacred? What have we made into gods and then served? What have we done in the name of filling our empty selves up? As soon as I began to overturn these stones and look at what was beneath them, I began to see my character defects in a very glaring light. The answers come quickly, much more quickly than our answers to *What do I believe?* We have held sacred money, power, success, anything we could call proof of our worth. We have invested meaning in meaningless things and then collected them like children collect rocks at the shore. We have chased love for the having rather than the giving; we have sought praise for doing what we should have done in the first place; we have clutched that praise and that love in our fists and called it *mine*.

And we have believed—it's been one of our central, guiding beliefs—that any and all of these things would bring us happiness. Once we just had *this,* then happiness would come rushing into our lives, to stay. Pain and struggle would be forever absent, *if only I had . . .*

If we have been spiritually hungry, we will not be filled by any of that. Some would say we can only be spiritually fulfilled by a God or some external cosmic force. I believe fulfillment may come from finding our spiritual sources here in the world, in each other, in ourselves, in the connections we build—and in all that we give. And in order to give, we need to examine our values, our moral structures, and see if they are really aligned with the needs of others and with the world's need. This is the desire to live rightly in the world, as a person of moral strength and development, as someone who becomes ever more spiritually vital and alive.

The great peace that comes with recognizing one's humanity—the peace that comes with the spiritual awakening of humility—is the peace that guides us through our moral quagmires, through the moral mess we've made and the considerable mess we often are. It accompanies us, nudging us to laugh at ourselves, reminding us that we are human and, as such, are flawed. The process of moral evolution is endless, and not painless. But it can be peaceful, if we allow our spiritual wisdom—our humility, our honesty, our willingness—to guide us. *Twelve Steps and Twelve Traditions* calls humility "the avenue to true freedom of the human spirit" (page 73). And it may well be right.

Steps Six and Seven are often brushed off, especially by the nonbeliever, because they seem to assume a direct relationship with a personal God. But they really are essential, and reconceptualizing them in a way that allows us to reach their spiritual core—the development of a clear moral self—is crucially important to those of us working the Steps in sobriety.

As a practical matter, it comes down to the fact that if we do not face and deal with our character defects—those things that interfere with our usefulness to the world, those things that lack moral worth, and those things that kept us addicted—we will in all likelihood relapse. The refusal to morally grow is a refusal to spiritually grow, and if we do not allow spiritual growth, we will stay trapped in the very same moral and spiritual wasteland where only our addiction thrived. I tried very hard to skip these Steps, to say, *Yes, of course, I have character defects, everyone does,* and to move on as quickly as possible without looking too hard at those defects, where they came from, what they were, or how they were wreaking havoc in my own and others' lives. In truth, what I believed deep down was that I was incapable of developing a moral structure that would allow me to live honestly and carefully and generously in the world. I believed I had no moral code at all. This was why I didn't want to look at myself or try to work these Steps. I thought it best to simply skip them and go on to the more obviously action-oriented matter of making amends.

There's little point in making amends—in trying to set things right between yourself and the world—when you don't have the moral wherewithal to examine what you believe to be right in the first place. I tried to skip these Steps and go on to ones I liked better. And I got drunk.

So I tried again. This time, I spent a long, long time thinking about what I meant by moral, what I saw as moral in other people and how that could teach me, what I believed my own life needed to be in order to reflect my moral and spiritual beliefs. Finally, I realized that the Steps themselves were not at all closed off to the nonbeliever. Step Six—Were entirely ready to have God remove all these defects of character—simply asks us to be ready for change. We do not have to believe in a personal, intervening God in order to make ourselves morally, spiritually ready for a transformation in our core beliefs. Step Seven—Humbly asked Him to remove our shortcomings—actually just asks us to *wait*. We wait for guidance, which we trust will arrive—perhaps not from a God on High, but from the spiritual wisdom we gather around us and the spiritual wisdom within, which we are learning to hear and which speaks up in its own time. We wait.

There is literature common to the Twelve Step program that says the ultimate goal of Steps Six and Seven is "spiritual and moral perfection." Here I depart from the literature. It seems to me that a quest for perfection flies in the face of an awareness of one's humanity and the need for humility. So then what *are* we trying to achieve in this work?

We're not. We're not trying to achieve anything or arrive anywhere. This path does not lead to an end point. This is the essence of the spiritual process—ongoing growth, gradual transformation, the changing spectrum of the spiritual self over the course of a life.

We are only here a moment. There is nothing we need to chase any longer, nor is there anything we need to run from. Now we can simply walk the path of our lives. The fullness of our lives comes not in their static achievements but in their constant transformations. And the fullness of a spiritual life comes from our willingness to undergo that transformation, to change, to be changed—by what we go through, by the actions we take, by the gradual arrival of spiritual wisdom and moral strength. Steps Six and Seven ask us to make ourselves entirely open to that process of change and to wait for that change to manifest in our conscious lives.

Each of the Steps has brought us closer to this point where we deepen our own willingness to change into morally conscious, spiritually awake people. The Steps we'll take next put that moral and spiritual vitality to work in the world.

❧

CHAPTER SEVEN

Healing

Harvest (August and September)

*There comes a moment in the spiritual life cycle when we are prepared to
reap the rewards of developing spiritual integration and strength, asking
spiritual questions and coming to meaningful answers, and making decisions that have sparked spiritual movement in our lives. Often we have
asked, What is the source of comfort, without God? And here we become
deeply aware of the capacity we have to heal ourselves and to be healed by
going through the painful but necessary process of facing damage we have
done. This process develops in us honesty, humility, and awareness of the
spiritual needs of others, without which we cannot be fully spiritual ourselves. No longer running from what we have chosen in the past, we are able
to choose differently in the present and to finally live according to the beliefs
that we hold. We have come to Steps Eight and Nine.*

Here is my map: well worn, torn into pieces, a jigsaw of places I've been.
This is the map of my past. As year turned into year, the map became ever
more ragged as I tore across the landscape of my life. Finally I've slowed
down and can breathe. And now, much as I long to look only ahead, I need
to turn around, go back, and repair what I've done. I need to repair who I
am. I need to heal what I can.

So I lay the map out on the table. I tape it together. I take my red pen and
trace the path I need to walk, a path that leads from this place where I am,
a place of new peace, and takes me back. South and west, down freeways
and backcountry highways, through prairies and mountains, crisscrossing

desert and ocean, into cities and small towns. I took this path here, and now I need to retrace my steps.

I mark the points on the map where damage was done. I circle swaths of scorched earth, collapsed structures, the wreckage of places I left behind in my haste to get the hell away from the messes I'd made. And as I make this plan for a journey in reverse, I try to remember. I peer closer at the map to make out names and faces that I've forgotten, whether because of the passage of time or because of my own willful amnesia. I hadn't noticed until now how much I've erased and hadn't grasped how much needs to be filled in.

And it must be filled in if I am to keep what I've found—a measure of serenity, a place of peace, an ever-stronger sense of spiritual wholeness. I will lose these things if I don't go back and look at where I was and who I was to this world. If I don't revisit the points on my journey here—if I do not look at how I became the addict I became, how I lost sight of my spiritual self, how that lack of spiritual integrity caused me to live—I will be pulled back into the confusion and chaos from which I've finally emerged.

I would like to begin again, here and now. I'd like to swallow the pieces of this map and not look back, or ever look in the eyes of people I've hurt, or ever hear what they might like to say to me now. Part of me insists that to do this is simply to rip open old wounds, and demands to know what good that is now. Let bygones be bygones, etc. But the truth is that those wounds are still open. I just try not to look at them, not to feel the sting that sometimes shoots through me when I am reminded of something I'd like to forget. Those wounds will not heal if I pretend they aren't there.

South and west. Away from this place I've come to rest, away from the settled, easy sense that I'm finally safe—and the occasional uneasy sense that I've escaped something and left it undone. Down twisting roads, through tangled streets, around corners I turned in desperation or fear. Out of my peaceful present and into the past, the now-unfamiliar places from which I alienated myself, places that now seem like someone else's world, someone else's life. Back to the person who seems, in fact, like someone else but is not.

I leave the quiet house by the lake and take the trip I've forgotten, but know by heart. Back to the winter street where I sat drunk in the snow, staring into the dregs of the bottle, the last drink I'd take. The endless string of rooms I occupied and abandoned, and the people who lived there with me, who watched me rage, go silent, and leave. The people stung by my harsh words. The people who were left to clean up. Back to the broken door frame, the holes kicked in the windshield and the wall. The notes on kitchen counters, *Sorry. Bye.* The cities so long since erased I do not know how to find my own street.

So I wander until I find it. I get lost, double back, go in circles, until things look familiar, until I find myself standing in front of the San Francisco liquor store above which I lived. Then I stumble on the coffee shop where I said something I should never have said. I pass my own reflection in a shop window and see myself as I was, as I am.

I sit down at a table outside that coffee shop with a friend. It's the only hot season in this city by a chilly bay. The wind that blows up off the bay into the hills is the only thing that cools the beating sun on the skin. My friend and I sit in the noise of the city for a while.

"I'm sorry," I finally say.

She drinks her coffee.

I say, "I want to make it right if I can."

She studies me. Not warmly, she replies, "Don't ever do that again. Not ever again."

"All right," I say.

And the slow process of healing begins.

—

The process of spiritual healing is a process of healing the breakages in our lives, the rifts in our relationships, and the open wounds in ourselves. One of these areas is not sufficient. Going around trying to tape together our relationships and our lives before we've done our inner work will be useless; by the same token, our inner work, the process of healing our own emotional pain, does not become a fully spiritual process until we heal our relationship with the world.

The spirituality that makes sense to me is one in which I am able to finally be at peace with myself, with others, and with what I am doing in my life, each day. My spiritual voice speaks clearest when I am at this peace; it is a peace that comes when the connection between myself and the world is not broken by my addiction, my moral incongruities, my refusal to give or receive. At peace, I am able to connect on a deep and fulfilling level in my relationships, as I never was when I was deaf to my spiritual self. At peace, I am able to do work in the world that is meaningful to me, and hopefully beyond me—whether that be the work I do for a living, or the work of feeding my own friendships as they need to be fed, or the work of taking action and being of service to something greater and in more need than I am myself.

But this peace does not come—though I've often wished it would—while I sit alone trying to bandage my own wounds. It does not come from trying to forget. It doesn't come from erasing what I've done or what I've felt was done to me. The spiritual healing I've sought has only been found by beginning to heal how I have related to the world. Until I do all I can to heal those I've harmed, to repair the places where I have done damage, I won't have any way of knowing how to avoid doing damage again. Until I face how my relationship to the world has really been, I will never know the truth of who I was, nor will I know who I am now. And until I know those things—who I was, who I am—I will never become the person I want to be. I will not become an active expression of my own spiritual self.

This stage of spiritual development is one where we wake up, often suddenly, to the startling daybreak of life in the world. I'd been sitting in the small dark room of my own despair so long that I'd forgotten what daylight was like, and I had become quite certain I would never see it again. I believed the effort it would take for me to find my way to it would be far too painful, and I didn't feel I had the strength to even try. What I feared, above all, was looking into the faces of those I'd loved and hurt, and seeing that hurt in their eyes. I didn't want to see pain I'd caused. I didn't want to see anger. I didn't want to see judgment. I thought of these things and curled into a ball.

I've wondered since if perhaps I thought they wouldn't *notice* that I'd hurt them, if I never looked them in the eye. Perhaps I thought my endless departures would leave a puff of smoke in my wake, rather than the ever-increasing pile of wreckage I actually trailed. But the very idea of sitting down over a cup of coffee and giving someone the opportunity to speak and to tell me what, if anything, I could do to make it right, was more terrifying than almost anything. Anything but the idea of a drink.

So I was between a rock and a hard place: On one side, the mountain of amends I'd need to scale if I wanted to set my relationships and my life in the human community right. On the other side, certain and rapid destruction in the form of a bottle. I chose the mountain.

Though I'd been told time and again by wise people who knew already what lay on the other side, I couldn't imagine what kind of peace or what degree of spiritual growth was waiting for me after my climb. The world opens up. The shadows fall. Daylight finally floods in.

And I was no longer alone.

Prior to beginning this phase of spiritual healing, part of me was certain that retracing my steps to these places and people who brought painful memories to the surface would have the opposite effect: I believed fervently that if people knew what I'd done (as if they didn't know—of course they knew), if I put it into words, if I just *spoke*, they'd look at me in shock and disgust and simply walk away.

Of course, many of them already had. The funniest thing that happened during this process—and there were actually a lot of funny things—was an old friend calling me up out of nowhere and saying furiously, "Don't you dare get in touch with me and make those amends or whatever they're called." And then he hung up.

Fair enough. Far stranger was the reaction of many others with whom I needed to reconnect and repair what I could. A surprising number of people looked at me in curiosity and said, "What?" They hadn't known I was hauling around this guilt and shame because, in several cases, they had no idea what I was talking about. Others knew what I was talking about and were simply glad to have it all out in the open. Others were angry, and said so. Each person had a unique response; that was his or her business. It was not my business to tell people how to feel. I'd been trying to do that for years. It is a particularly egregious form of trying to control what is beyond our control. Other people's hearts and minds are not ours to manage and manipulate. But I tried. And to no good effect.

So part of this process is, again, letting go. We let go here of the need and the attempt to make people do and feel what we wish. We allow them to own their own hearts. We let go of all the masks we've held up to hide ourselves, masks we hoped would make us someone worth love and respect. At this point, we have done enough work on ourselves to trust, in some measure, that we are worthy of strong relationships and the spiritual nourishment they bring. So it's safe to let down the mask, to let someone leave our lives if that is what they choose to do, to let them say their piece and to accept the power of their feeling, to let go of our faulty notion that relationships are a game in which we keep score. Ultimately, what we are doing here is stepping back to see this person, these people, for who they are and allowing them to see us as human, flawed, and also whole as well.

In this letting go, there is a wellspring of healing. By seeing others for who they are—and not for who they are to us or how we hope they'll see us—we learn to relate to them on a spiritual level, which can't be done when we see in them only a reflection of who we are. This heals an enormous amount of damage that we've done to others and to ourselves, to our concept of the human contract, to our very concepts of respect and love. It was not until I began to see others as they were that I was able to fully appreciate and see the beauty in them. And until I learned to see the beauty in the people around me, I was lacking an enormous piece of my spiritual life. I was lacking any real understanding of love.

And ultimately, my spirituality does center on the human capacity for love. Not on some outer Force of Love somewhere in the universe—but on the astonishing ability all of us have within ourselves to love one another and to act in the world based on that love. My addiction had blocked off my ability to feel love even within myself, let alone see it in others. I had long since stopped knowing how to love people well; the process of spiritual healing was, in great part, the process of learning how to love again.

That relearning included the work of seeing the people in my life with new eyes. People I had lost, people I had hurt, people I had meant to love but had not known how—I needed to go back to them and show them this love now. No matter how angry I was with them—that anger had to be set down. No matter how I felt they had harmed me—that hurt in me would not be healed until I took care of repairing my part. I was going to need to forgive, a form of love with which I had precious little familiarity.

And one thing I had not expected when I set out: I would need to learn—however silly it sounds—to forgive and to love myself. Despite all I'd done. Despite my anger with myself. Despite shame. If I was going to try to heal the rifts in my relationships and in my life, I was going to need to heal myself as well, to see myself with the respect I was ready to offer others, to forgive my human errors. The process of spiritual healing includes the moment when we forgive ourselves for our pasts and allow ourselves to move forward at last.

What I was sure would be a ripping open of old wounds became, as I worked on repairing my relationships, quite the opposite. I realized that those wounds had been open all along and would never be healed until I truly attended to each one. The things that had held me back from making restitution to a very long list of people—my own ego, fear, a powerful desire to escape the necessary pain of growth, and a frantic wish to escape myself—were things that flew in the face of my spiritual needs. When I reached this stage of my journey, I had had plenty of experience with ego, escapism, and fear, and very little experience tapping into my own strength and capacity to heal.

For those of us who have asked ourselves, *Without a God, what comforts me? What heals?* the realization that this healing can be found at the precise intersection of our own lives with the lives of others is an essential one. This is the "end of isolation" spoken of in *Twelve Steps and Twelve Traditions*. I had never before realized that without others, without *giving* to others, I could not myself be healed. It came as a shock to understand that until I reached out to another person, my spiritual life would never be strong or very deep. Until we are asked to give—until we are asked to heal a wound in someone else, even if that wound is one we inflicted ourselves—we cannot receive the healing that we, too, need.

It doesn't matter, really, whether or not we are forgiven by others. That guilt and shame that has eaten away at so many of us for years warps us, preventing us from either feeling or giving love and making it impossible for us to do our work in the world. We cannot see past the guilt and shame that we've held on to and so cannot see others clearly enough to know them. But it *is* our work in the world to know others; it is our spiritual work to reach out to them and offer all that we can.

And in this case, what we can offer is not another iteration of the same tired apology, but a new, real, undisguised self. The spiritually alive self we have been uncovering in our work so far is a very different person than we were before. We have set down whatever poison was silencing our spirits and destroying our bodies and minds. We have recognized our own insanity and come to the belief that sanity will be restored by spiritual work. We are learning to let go of our fear and the desperate drive to control what it creates. We have taken a close look at ourselves and our lives; we know ourselves better and are no longer blindly lashing out in fear, anger, and pain. We have begun to explore our moral beliefs and to live by them. So the people we are now, retracing our steps through our lives, are possessed of strength, self-knowledge, and an enormous capacity for forgiveness and love.

The fact that we know we're new does not mean anyone else knows that. It isn't our job to force that knowledge on them. There's no need to prove a point. There's no undoing all the apologies and promises we've made before, and we are in no position to demand forgiveness and trust. Part of repairing our relationships is allowing the people in our lives to do what they need to do. One of the things people will need to do is see us living our lives differently, if they choose to stay in our lives at all. This takes time, and there's no forcing it. It took many years for the people closest to me to see that I was different and that the changes in my life reflected deeper changes in myself. Spiritual changes do not come with bells and whistles, and I've never known them to come with bolts of lightning either. They start slow and evolve, working their way from our dormant inner selves to the point where we are now, finally reaching out to others, finally seeing *them*.

This is truly our time to see others—not their time to see us. The purpose of this phase in the process is not to perform. Rather, the purpose is to expand our humility, to let go of fear and ego and all that blocks us from our spiritual selves, to set down the weight of the past that we've carried for so long, and to deepen our understanding of respect and love. I cannot say I'd really learned to do any of those things very well until I went back and did what I could to repair my life. It was in offering that respect and love to those I'd hurt most that I was most healed.

This time in our spiritual lives is one we may fear most, but one that is essential to our spiritual development in another way. When we go back to the very beginning—to the earliest sources of hurt, the places where our addiction burrowed in and took root—and walk the path we've taken in our lives, looking with clear eyes at the places we've been, at the faces we've known, we are finally able to become integrated people. By the time I came to sobriety, I felt like my life was a shattered bottle on the floor, an unintelligible scattering of shards that I could never possibly put back together in order to see my life, my self, as a whole. But when I fully engaged with this stage of my spiritual life, I began to piece together what my addiction had smashed.

The spiritual self is the deepest, most integrated aspect of who we are. And in doing this work, traveling this road that seemed both foreign and strangely familiar, I felt my spiritual self begin to come to life in a way it had not done before. I began to see the truth of what I'd been told: it would not be possible to have a fully spiritual experience until my past had been cleaned up, my heart cleared of its wreckage, the damage I'd done in the world repaired. I was simply carrying too much. It was in going back that I was finally able to feel myself move forward with strength and without the burden I'd been carrying for so long.

In piecing our lives together, in learning what our own stories are, for good and for ill, we become whole. This transformation can only take place when we connect with others. I went around for a very long time possessed of the notion that my life was *my* life—that I was an isolated creature, answerable to and responsible only for myself. While this is an exceedingly easy way to live, insofar as it requires of us no action in the world, the isolation it creates is enormous, and isolation is a kind of pain that the human heart can't tolerate for long. Our lives wither when they are not brought into relationship with other lives, when our spirits are not asked to nourish and comfort other human spirits, when we are allowed to believe that we are truly alone. We require relationships not only as comfort; we require them in order to survive and to grow. The stagnation so many of us have seen in ourselves, in our lives and our spirits, was due in great part to the isolation we chose and the isolation inflicted on us by our addiction. In this stagnant place, the spirit starves.

Am I ultimately alone? How many of us have asked that question—drunk or sober—when we've wondered if there was a God or when we've decided that there was none? And the universe reels around us, more vast than we could begin to comprehend and more apparently empty. But it's only when we overlook the fairly obvious fact that we are *human beings on a planet packed with human beings* that we can entertain the fairly self-indulgent idea that we are, in fact, alone. The idea that I was alone was one I held firmly in my most deeply addicted, deeply isolated years. I was projecting my spiritual deadness onto a world filled with spiritual life, a world full of spiritual need, and a world requiring both my work and my love. By clinging to my belief that I was alone, I managed to avoid both doing that work and learning to love.

But when we stumble upon the realization that we are nothing like alone, we also realize, with some alarm, that we have *never* been alone—and that we have been *acting* as if we have been alone for many years. As we become aware of our own responsibility to live as an interconnected part of the human community, we also become painfully aware that our belief that we were alone has caused us to behave in a way that was not responsible to that community, was not respectful of the humanity of others, even of those we said we loved. We become aware that we have not fully loved. And our own histories sometimes smack us in the face.

Those histories—fractured, fragmented, out of any discernible order—are the place where we begin. We can't just start over; if we do, we are missing an integral piece of our own stories and selves, and we are neglecting responsibility, as many of us have always done. We are also denying ourselves the critical opportunity to see people as they truly are; and until we bear witness to the people we have loved, we will not know how to bear witness to the people we will love in the future. We will not know how to bring clear eyes into the world where we will do our work. We will not know how to see the beauty and grace in the human lives we want to touch.

At this point in a process of spiritual growth, we begin to own ourselves and our lives. We take responsibility for our errors and accept our own humanity and that of others. Gradually, we begin to lose the sense that our lives are completely out of control; we are held steady now by a conscious effort to live rightly in the world. The sense that we are strangers to ourselves begins to fade, as well; less and less often do we find ourselves acting in ways that are out of alignment with our moral and spiritual principles. This is the journey of healing—we heal the relationships we've had as best we can; we heal the rifts in our lives; and we heal the wounds left in us. The ragged edges of our spirits, where addiction tore us out of the human community, begin to repair, and the spiritual experience of reentering the world—where we are not and were never alone—begins.

It is in its discussion of Steps Eight and Nine that the Big Book says, "The spiritual life is not a theory. *We have to live it*" (page 83). It emphasizes the fact that while the actions we are taking here are partly to set our lives in order, the ultimate purpose of doing that is to make ourselves useful to others and, in doing so, to deepen our spiritual lives. While these Steps can look, at first, like a horrifying and possibly pointless slog through a past we'd much rather abandon, they are actually an essential phase of spiritual growth.

And they are, for many people, the most feared and most often skipped-over Steps in the Twelve Step program. Many people, myself included, have argued with themselves, with sponsors, with people in meetings, about whether certain amends were actually necessary. Ego, pride, and fear fly up as defenses against having to actually make contact with people we've harmed. Those things need to be stepped over as we move forward with our amends. This is where the oft-cited line "we would go to any lengths for victory over alcohol" is found in the Big Book (page 76). We need this healing. Our spirits will not evolve in the future if the past is not set right.

Nor will our relationships ever be strong. It is only in an examination of the relationships we've had—and those that have somehow survived our addiction—that we learn where we've made mistakes and learn how not to make them as we go forward. We've been, as the Big Book says, like tornadoes ripping through the lives of others. The only way to change that pattern is to look honestly at what we've done, make restitution wherever we possibly can, and begin to act according to the spiritual principles that we now want to guide our lives.

So what are the spiritual principles that we want guiding us as we interact with others? I can think of a few that are, to me, indispensable: Love, *agape*, the Greek word that means love of all. Generosity: giving all that we have, giving from the bottomless spiritual well. Empathy: another kind of giving, a giving of the open heart. Honesty: a way of giving the true self. Acceptance: giving people the freedom to be who they are. These are only a few of the spiritual principles we now put into practice, and they are ones we continue to practice over time. They deepen our spiritual connection to others and strengthen our own spiritual lives.

The capacity to put these principles into practice arises from the work we've done in Steps Six and Seven, the careful thought we've put into what our moral foundations really are and what we want them to be as we go forward. In looking at my past, I had to recognize that my behavior in relationships bore no resemblance to the beliefs I held about who I should be and how I should live. When I was still in active addiction, my "morals" were a sort of nebulous, free-floating ideal that had no real connection to my life on the ground. It was in doing this phase of spiritual work that I began to apply my own values to myself. That continues to be a necessary area of effort for me and for most recovering people I know; the spiritual life, as the Big Book says, is not a theory. It has to be lived. And it is lived out, first and foremost, in our relationships.

Knowing the spiritual foundations that we want undergirding our interaction with others, we can make our amends for not having lived according to those principles in the past. Not everyone will see, or care, that we have changed; that's not the point. The point is to open a spiritual connection that our addiction had closed. If the other person chooses to meet us on a spiritual level, great. If not, that works too. Our work is only to be willing, to be honest, and to open our hearts. This is the only way a relationship can be healed, and even if that relationship is lost, it is the only way to heal ourselves.

So we put away our ego and our pride, and take up humility and willingness instead. We make a thorough list of people to whom we need to make amends, and we go down that list one by one. It's not going to work to pick and choose, doing only the easy ones, telling ourselves this one or that one simply can't be made—there is always something we can do that puts our spiritual approach to relationships into action, whether that means sitting down with someone who is still in our lives or writing a letter to someone who is no longer accessible to us. I burned a whole lot of bridges, so I wrote a whole lot of letters to people who fervently hoped never to see me again. Some I sent, some I did not; it's essential, in making amends, to remain aware of the part of Step Nine that reads "except when to do so would injure them or others." I found it necessary to repeatedly get the guidance of a sponsor when making these judgment calls. But if we hope for a true spiritual experience, we need to do this work wholeheartedly and without reservation. The spiritual rewards of this Step are many, and it would be foolish to reap only a few.

As time goes on, it's become clear to me that the past unfolds itself a little at a time, showing me things about my history, my relationships, my morals, and myself gradually rather than all at once. The willingness I have needed to make some amends has not come right away in every case; in some cases, that willingness didn't come for a decade, and in some cases I didn't realize I needed to make an amend until well into sobriety. The task is to remain open to these realizations about our relationships and our actions in the world. When we are doing strong spiritual work in all areas of our lives, that openness begins to come naturally. Willingness becomes a way of life; humility grows with time.

And these are two of the things that bring us to the serenity, the peace of mind, and the real spiritual experience so many people feel at this point in their work through the Steps. In the Big Book, we arrive here at The Promises:

> If we are painstaking about this phase of our development, we will be amazed before we are halfway through. We are going to know

a new freedom and a new happiness. We will not regret the past nor wish to shut the door on it. We will comprehend the word serenity and we will know peace. No matter how far down the scale we have gone, we will see how our experience can benefit others. That feeling of uselessness and self-pity will disappear. We will lose interest in selfish things and gain interest in our fellows. Self-seeking will slip away. Our whole attitude and outlook upon life will change. Fear of people and of economic insecurity will leave us. We will intuitively know how to handle situations which used to baffle us.

The Promises conclude, "We will suddenly realize that God is doing for us what we could not do for ourselves" (pages 83–84). For those of us who do not believe in a God, the recognition that spiritual work—work on our own innermost lives and the development of our connection to others and to the larger world—is "doing for us what we could not do for ourselves" is no less significant. I for one could not have imagined my own capacity for healing, nor could I have imagined that it would take a spiritual connection to the world to truly heal me. I never knew that a spiritual life, or a spiritual experience of any kind, would be possible for me; I did not believe in a God, and I still believed a God was required in order to have a spiritual life.

I know now that I find the depth of spirituality in my connection to others, in my work in the world, and in an ongoing practice of spiritual growth. That ongoing practice—which I believe exists in the simplest moments of our day-to-day life—brings us to Step Ten.

CHAPTER EIGHT

###

Spiritual Practice

October

Having risked much for the serenity and spiritual strength we have begun to feel, and having explored the wordless landscape of the heart in all its seasons, we have brought our spiritual selves into alignment with the world in which we live. Long cut off from both inner spirit and outer world by our own will, ego, lack of trust, and fear of the unknown, we now need to develop a regular practice of spiritual maintenance that involves the engagement of both others and self. The spirituality we have been discovering is one that takes place and finds fullness here on the ground; our spiritual practice must then help us maintain our connection to the here and now, our responsibility to it, and our learning from it as well. A spiritual practice here and now keeps our lives in balance with others, helps us maintain our own serenity, and restores our spirit so that we have more to give in this world. We have come to Step Ten.

Autumn rushes into the city on a sharp wind, spinning whorls of just-fallen leaves down the streets. The trees are a kaleidoscope of color, an explosion of pinks and oranges and yellows and reds. In the late afternoon, I shove my hands into my pockets and walk, under an improbably blue sky, up the hill, around the lake, and through the neighborhoods to the steps of the church where I go to my Tuesday meeting. I do this weekly, have been doing it for more than a decade. But this afternoon, the air seems clearer, the smells of lake water and dry leaves are more precise, and somehow the clutter of the city falls away more quickly than usual. And I find myself thinking about that Tuesday, ten years ago, when I suddenly realized that I had—after a long time away—returned to the world.

It was not a remarkable day—autumn, as it is now, and lovely, like today. I'd bundled myself into my usual oversized hooded sweatshirt and come scuffling up the walk of the church. I'd nodded curtly to the people at the meeting who kept insisting upon saying hello to me, despite my scowl and my refusal to meet their eyes. I'd spent the bulk of the meeting staring at the floor, listening hard, as I had since the first time I'd walked in. I'd gone to the meeting for the first time in June, barely sober, and for all those months had managed to say nothing more than my name and the fact that I was an alcoholic when introductions came around to me. And still, people kept smiling at me, saying hello. I half-wondered what was wrong with them.

All summer, I'd had the strangest feeling that I was invisible. That I made no sound when I walked, wasn't really there at all. Since the moment I got sober, I felt as though I'd entered another world, where everything was clear, piercingly vivid, solid, and *real*, but that in this world I couldn't quite place myself. I felt fragile, maybe not totally tangible, maybe a figment of my own imagination. When the people at the meeting spoke to me, I was startled every time. I stammered out my clumsy hellos, chewed on my fingernails, and hoped they'd talk to someone else soon.

That October Tuesday, the meeting began as it usually did—everyone else visible, me invisible in my chair. And then a funny thing happened. The person who was supposed to speak hadn't shown up. So, the group leader asked, did anyone else want to take the person's spot? Anyone have anything to say on the Tenth Step?

I heard someone say, "I'll talk."

I looked around. Everyone was staring at me. I stared at them. Then I realized I was the one who'd spoken. And, in a rush, I understood that I was visible, had a presence, took up space, made a sound, was *sober*, was in fact *alive*.

A little distracted by this new information, I started to talk. I talked and talked. I talked to the ceiling, I talked to the floor—didn't meet a lot of eyes—but I talked, because it was time. I'd come this far. I might as well open the door of the world and finally step in.

"We have entered the world of the Spirit," it says in the Big Book, when we get to Step Ten (page 84). That night, as I walked home under a heavy yellow harvest moon, I realized it was true. This is the world of the spirit. This world, as it is, this crowded earthbound heaven, here and now.

The world of the spirit, the one in which we live, is the present place where we stand. Here is where we can find our spiritual nourishment, and here is where we must give back. The most salient fact of this spiritual world, the starkest difference between this world and our old world of addiction, is this: we are not the only ones here. This world of the spirit is thickly populated with people. Where we lived before in absolute isolation, now we live in context. This is none other than what we always longed for, always lacked: a community of which we can be, and must be, an integral, active part. We must live out our spiritual lives here, tangled up with and touching these infinite other lives.

What is a spiritual life? A *life* lived in the world of the spirit—not only brief forays into that world, not only isolated moments of spiritual awareness? How do we build our days on a foundation of spiritual awareness? How do we allow spiritual principles to guide our actions? How do we keep ourselves mindful of this spiritual world around and within us—how do we stay truly present to this place—rather than slipping back out the door into the spiritually empty world with which we're so familiar? What keeps us here and now, growing and continuously aware?

A spiritual life is one lived in that awareness and growth. It takes an infinite number of forms. The practices we choose for ourselves that keep us closely attuned to our spiritual voices will differ; some of them we will discover by accident, some we must seek out. But I know that for myself, and for the people I've seen who have the serenity I admire, this much is necessary: I must be continuously aware of my interactions with the world. I am not alone here. I am not answerable only to myself anymore. I am not, it turns out, invisible. And so at this stage in my spiritual development, I have to carefully attend to how I move in the world. I am not the only one making my way.

This is the world that I live in, and this is the world that I love—crowded, clattering, packed to the rafters with people, each of whom has a story, each of whom carries an entire history and also an ever-changing nebula of dreams, fears, hopes, and needs. I spent most of my life entirely oblivious to these other lives, and utterly unaware that I had any impact on them. I stormed through my life, blind to what or who I walked on, unwilling to admit it when I realized I'd caused harm. This is no way to live. This is no way, either, to love. And until I learn to love, I cannot have any hope of staying spiritually alive.

The spiritual work we've done—waiting through doubt and despair, unfurling into hope and discovery, coming into full flower, and now arriving at the moment where we begin to truly reap the rewards of that work—is not work we do once and then stop. These are simply points in time, moments in a spiritual life; we have only made a beginning. The ultimate reward of this work is not some white-light moment, not a conclusion of any kind. The reward of this work *is* a spiritual life. The reward is entrance to the "world of the Spirit," which is to say, entrance to *this* world, a place at this table, in this human life. I am not much concerned about the existence of a hereafter, a "next" life—this life is what I have, this is where I live, and I believe that my spiritual growth depends upon the work I do here and now. That work amounts to seeing this world clearly, moving through it gently, and learning to love it well.

The times of spiritual harvest in our lives are times when we feel the richness of life in all its seasons—when we feel the effects of work we have done as well as an awareness of the work that lies ahead. This is when spiritual practice becomes possible. We are no longer in a moment of desolation, wrung dry, spiritually bereft; we have new riches of spiritual growth within us and can put those stores of spiritual wealth to use. This is the time when we can take what we have found out into the world, and we do it in a very simple way: we watch where we step.

This seems a tiny way of loving the world, but it is where we begin. The spiritual practice of taking responsibility for our actions puts us in a position of constantly seeing, and appreciating, the world in which we live and the people who live in it with us. As I do my daily work of walking carefully among others, I am able to finally see who they are, what they may need, what I may have to offer them. This deepens my gratitude for them, and allows me all the awe at their beauty and respect for their humanity that I need to really love them well. Until this time in my life—until I'd done the spiritual work that brought me here—I never knew how to love. I am only learning now.

Tuesday, October, on my way to the meeting where I first realized I was alive in the world. I stop at the neighborhood coffee shop, get a cup of coffee, and sit down at a table outside in a blustery wind that sends leaves spinning around my feet. I am surrounded by clusters of chattering, gesturing, laughing people. There are shocked-looking babies in tiny hats, cheerful ridiculous dogs, old men in too-high pants taking their Tuesday constitutional, young couples, solitary readers of books.

This, today, on a city sidewalk—*this* is the world of the spirit. This is my life, taking place in the same second as all these other lives, surrounded on all sides by other lives, my story intersected at all possible points by others' stories, my voice never an echo, my visibility always a fact. I sit quietly tangled up in the slipstream of this moment, sipping my coffee, grateful beyond measure, madly in love with it all.

The sound of our cacophony—the inelegant, jumbled-up, glorious human song—is caught by the cold wind, spun in its fingers, and whipped down the street.

—

As the Big Book says, "We have entered the world of the Spirit. Our next function is to grow in understanding and effectiveness" (page 84). Upon realizing that the spiritual work we've done so far has brought us to an entirely new place in our lives, we encounter our next task: the development of a healthy relationship with the human community of which we are a part. Many of us have been totally unprepared for this task until now. It's required every Step we've taken so far to gain the strength, insight, and depth of feeling we need. These things are necessary for a strong, deeply felt, consistent spiritual practice, a way of living spiritually in the world. The "effectiveness" of which the Big Book speaks is an effective way of moving through our lives, which are inextricably bound up with the lives of others; to grow in effectiveness, then, we will need to grow in our ability to connect with those we encounter.

Bringing spiritual awareness into our daily lives is how we do that. We become effective participants in the human community by being integrated human beings ourselves, by living our days in a place of continuous spiritual consciousness, building our actions on an ethical foundation, and continuing to grow in our own spiritual strength. I have lived much of my life divorced from my spiritual self, and that removal of the spiritual from my daily existence was precisely what made me such a seriously ineffective participant in my own life, let alone in the larger world. I lived by vacillating wildly from head to heart, crashing through the world head-first or heart-first, my actions based in either an unfeeling aridity of intellect or a thoughtless flood of emotion. The work I need to do in sobriety draws me into balance, where I try to live spirit-first.

To me, spiritual awareness is synonymous with a constant awareness of others, and of the world in which I take part. Becoming effective citizens of this "world of the Spirit" is, in some ways, a matter of being aware of one's location: Where am I standing? Who's nearby? How can I act in a way that will do no harm, and hopefully bring some good to them? Where are the people I love? What do they need from me now? When I need something from others, how can I go about getting it in a way that will take nothing away from someone else? Where are the people I do not know but who may have a need that I may be able to meet? How can I be of service? How do I need to feed my spirit so that I have something to offer?

The people I see living as effective members of this society are those who are not attempting to live unto and for themselves. The people whose lives seem ineffective to me are people who live like I used to—as if they are unaware of the noisy totality of everything around them and are studiously walking around with their hands over their ears wondering why they feel so alone. Effective membership in the human community amounts to a constant effort to retain one's consciousness of others and a willingness to care for others as one cares for oneself.

Does this come naturally to us? It didn't seem to come very naturally to me at first, and often enough I still have to remind myself that I live in context, not in isolation. But I know that as the days of active addiction move further into my past, I am more conscious of others and much less bothered with the nuisance noise of my greedier self. As the guiding principles of addiction fade—ego, want, resentment, fear—spiritual principles become the ones that guide my actions more often. Not always, by any stretch—that's the work of a lifetime, and it's the spiritual work I have to do.

Spiritual practice is how I habituate myself to an awareness that spiritual principles are the ones guiding me, informing my choices and behavior, choosing my words, showing me what is important and what is not as I go through my days. Those principles come up daily and require my attention—if I am to consider myself truly engaging in spiritual practice, I must be aware of my basic spiritual beliefs in willingness, honesty, humility, respect, and love. It's still a strange feeling, sometimes, even with some years of work on this under my belt; the vast majority of my life was spent out of touch with any spiritual sense and now I still feel a little inept at trying to live spirit-first. It's still much easier to live from my brain or from my emotional gut. But I've seen in my own life and in others' lives the wisdom of basing action in the spiritual principles that have meaning for us, and of working to make that a daily practice. So I keep at it.

And I have to. As soon as I stop, I'll slip backward. So far in this concentrated period of spiritual work, we've done an alarming number of major things—big decisions, personal inventories, emotional overhauls, difficult amends—that have moved us rapidly forward from spiritual death to a new and vital spiritual life. It can be tempting, at this point, to think we've pretty well made it over the hurdles we needed to clear to find freedom from addiction and enter to a different world. But that isn't the case. This, in truth, is where the real work begins. All this work we've done leads not to some far-off future point—it leads to here. Now. *Here, now* is where the spiritual work of our lives takes place.

Oddly, it can sometimes be easier to do the momentous, obviously difficult work, the kind that seems to lead to repeated epiphanies. The writer Anton Chekhov wrote marvelously, "Any idiot can face a crisis," and I'm often reminded of this when I think it's time to coast on the Big Stuff I think I've done. Some of us have lived from crisis to crisis for years and have acclimated to the constant roller coaster as a way of life. I certainly had, and when sobriety—and some measure of serenity—started to take root, I kept nervously looking around, wondering when things would get big and crashing again. It took a good long while for me to realize that spiritual practice didn't always involve enormous, earthshaking steps through old minefields; on the contrary, spiritual practice was mostly a matter of living consciously in the day to day. Sometimes people wonder, in truth, if they'll get bored; what's to keep us entertained without emotional mayhem and constant drama? Some of the stages of spiritual work feel equally monumental, and the changes in us feel just as massive. So it can be tempting to think that *that* is the nature of Real Spiritual Stuff—our version of white-light moments, discoveries, and shifts within the self.

But as best I can tell, Real Spiritual Stuff is found just as much in the small, careful work of living our days in spiritual awareness, getting steadily more familiar with our spiritual nature, as it exists in a continuous stream, and learning to align our beliefs with our actions, every day, regardless of what that day may bring. It's when I let up on daily spiritual practice—the active effort to live out my spiritual beliefs in all my doings and dealings with this present world—that I find myself back in crisis, handling it like the idiot I most certainly can be.

The people I see living out their spiritual beliefs make their whole lives a state of awareness—of themselves, of the world around them, and of their relations with that world. This is how they care for their own spiritual needs and use the peace of mind that comes from that constant upkeep to bring something good to others. I see them in constant practice, continuing to wear down the defenses and habits of heart and mind that shut them off from their spiritual selves, and so shut them off from true connection with the world. These defenses and habits are so long-standing in many of us that they seem hardwired by now; it takes a long time to break down the walls we've built within and outside ourselves. Not only do we have old walls to work on, we also have a nasty habit of throwing up new ones all the time. That's where the ongoing practice of spiritual awareness comes in. The split we have created over time between spirit and mind is one we've begun to repair in our work so far, but our work is truly only a beginning.

The divides we will again create in ourselves, and the ways in which we will shut ourselves off from others, are ones that will require our attention not once or twice, but from here on out.

And if we stop trying? If we settle in and get too comfortable with the notion that we've done all the big work, so we're all set? We slip backward, and a lot of us, not to put too fine a point on it, get drunk or high. Why?

The nature of addiction is retreat from the world. We slam doors as we go, walking further and further into the heart of a labyrinth for which we have no map and from which many people never emerge. In this retreat from the world, we quickly lose sight of other people—of their needs, of their nature, of their humanity—and we lose sight of our own, as well. We become fearful of the connections that once sustained us. We begin to hoard our emotional and spiritual energies for fear we'll run out. We lose faith in all we'd begun to trust, and we start holding onto things again, gathering up the burden we'd gratefully set down, hauling it with us as we remove ourselves from the world. All our old habits return, and our minds and emotions start to warp. Our spiritual lives dry up. Soon, we're stuck back in the heart of the labyrinth, quite alone.

This world of the spirit is, again, the world of context, the world of community. In order to stay in it, we need a spiritual practice. Perhaps our tendency to withdraw, to defend, to shut doors, is in our nature as people; perhaps it is in our acquired nature as addicts. Regardless, the only way to maintain our serenity and our sobriety, and to grow in human understanding and effectiveness, is to continue spiritual work. And that work takes place in the world.

So what does that look like? Some of the spiritual practices we choose for ourselves will differ from what other people do—as far as I can tell, they can be most anything, simply things that alert us to our spiritual voice and give us nourishment. But one that is indispensable to everyone I've seen who lives in ongoing spiritual growth is a practice of self-examination that focuses on how we are interacting with the world. This isn't navel-gazing. This is a serious, continuous awareness of how we treat others, how we respond to them, and how we give back.

This is where we put to use what we've learned so far—about action and self-knowledge, about awareness of the world beyond ourselves, and about our own moral and ethical beliefs. This is about how we want to live and who we want to be in the world. We are not examining here whether the world is giving enough to us or giving us the right things. We're looking at our own impact as we go through our days. This is a matter of aligning our beliefs with our actions, something not all of us have much experience with; I, at least, spent a lot of time thinking about how I wanted to be, how I wanted others to be, how I wanted *things* to be, and not a lot of time putting my money where my mouth was by examining my own behavior and living out my beliefs. The effort to become an ethical person, it turns out, is not an impossible ideal. It's a human responsibility. And it doesn't mean trying to be a saint. It means working toward integrity, an integration of action and belief.

So the trick is to keep watching for character defects and ethical inconsistencies (in *ourselves*, not in everyone else—something a lot of us are very good at). Someone I admire once told me that character defects amounted to "things that stand in the way of our usefulness to others," and that's a very straightforward, *practical* way of examining our behavior and our lives. My character defects consistently stand in the way of my being of any use to anyone else; every last one sucks me back into myself, my wishes, and my will. My job, then, is to keep an eye on those defects to see where they are interfering with my intentions—where my less spiritual side is getting between me and a peaceful, useful relationship with the world.

And when I see these character defects and inconsistencies of behavior coming up, what then? The Big Book says that in this situation, "we ask God to remove them." For a nonbeliever, the approach is the same here as it was in some of our earlier work: we let go of the thing we're holding on to that's triggering our character defects—whether that's fear, resentment, ego, or any of the long list of habits we've developed over time that interfere with our usefulness to others. When we look more deeply at ourselves, at the reasons we're behaving as we are, we'll always discover that old habits are springing up because we're hanging on to old emotional or spiritual baggage. So we let it go.

Then we take action. We need to immediately correct where we have been in the wrong. Amends may be necessary, certainly at least an acknowledgment of our part in a conflict or negative interaction. There may be times when our character defects are affecting mostly our own feelings—I, for example, get caught up in emotional stewing with annoying regularity—but that doesn't mean I'm not affecting other people. When my feelings are warped—when my spiritual and emotional life are out of balance—my behavior is affected, every time. So I can't afford to entertain my habit of stewing or any of the other ego-driven, fear-based, or resentment-wielding habits to which I'm prone. Instead, I have to swallow my pride, admit where I've been in the wrong, and offer to make it right if I can.

By doing this promptly and without fuss or drama, I prevent those slow fissures in my spiritual life—borne of acting in a way that is inconsistent with my beliefs—from widening into cracks, and then chasms, into which I'm bound to fall headfirst, doubtless dragging other people down with me. I also keep my amends list short.

Then, says the Big Book, as it goes through its suggestions for how to handle this kind of day-to-day spiritual practice, once our amends are made and our behavior examined for where we can make changes in the future, "we resolutely turn our thoughts to someone we can help" (page 84). This is an essential part of our active spiritual life in each day, a part of spiritual practice we can't afford to skip. First, it heals the spiritual wound we've actually caused *ourselves* by acting without integrity, no matter how small or large that self-inflicted wound may be. Second, it trains us to live with a constant awareness of the world beyond ourselves, an awareness that we are not living in isolation but in community, and a conviction that our individual spiritual maintenance can contribute to something larger than our own small lives.

It also trains us to lay down our arms. For people who've been fighting, fighting, fighting for so long—within ourselves, with others, with the world—an education in letting go of anger, taking responsibility for our own missteps and mistakes, is a crucial learning process. This line from the Big Book is one I hold particularly dear: "We have ceased fighting anything or anyone" (page 84). This line saves me from trying to control others (or the universe) or live by raging self-will. It reminds me to set down those character defects that are strongest in me. The realization that I am no longer at war with the world—that I am, rather, able to love it wholeheartedly, though my attempts to show this love sometimes are muddled—is an indescribable relief. I no longer gallop into each day brandishing my little sword, as I did for years. I just get up and go out into the world, do as much right as I can, fix all the things I do wrong as soon as I'm able, and feel an overwhelming gratitude that the war I was fighting is done.

And this is another Big Book line I love, one that comes in its discussion of this stage of spiritual work: "For by this time sanity will have returned" (page 84). When we examine our lives now, our spiritual lives, our ways of thinking, our behavior, our relationships, the truth of this statement is evident. The work we've done so far has brought us to the place that seemed impossibly far off only a little while ago, when we doubted that sanity could ever be ours. But we are here; this is the harvest we reap, this peace of mind, this serenity, this sanity in how we feel and how we live. The Promises we spoke of in the last chapter have begun to come true. This stage of our work, then, is about deepening our spiritual lives in a way we never could have done before sanity returned; and our spiritual lives must be deepened if we are to be of much use in the world.

For some people, at this point, there is a sense that their addiction has simply disappeared—some people would say it has been "lifted"—and I can attest to the sense that the obsession and compulsion surrounding addiction has faded into memory. No question, we are in a new place, in a new frame of mind, finally spiritually alive. But this may be the most important line in the Big Book, as I read it: "What we really have is a daily reprieve contingent on the maintenance of our spiritual condition" (page 85).

This *is* what we really have. The only way to keep the sanity we have obtained, the only way to grow in human understanding and effectiveness, is to develop a consistent set of daily spiritual practices that keep us free of all the habits of self that draw us back to our addicted lives. Daily practice, constant renewal, and ongoing spiritual work within ourselves and out in the world are required—not just recommended—to maintain the spiritual condition that grants us our reprieve. And we want not only to keep what we've found so far. We want to go further, and grow as spiritual people. With spiritual practice, we can.

The habit of self-examination this requires is still a new skill for many of us; some have never explored it before, some have let the habit lapse. We may be plenty familiar with self-absorption, self-pity, self-hatred, and self-flagellation; we may have spent many hours in thorough navel-gazing; we may have dabbled a little or a lot in self-directed rage and shame. But detached, judicious self-examination—simply looking at what's making us tick, what's triggering our character defects, and what's going on when our behavior gets out of alignment with our beliefs—may still be new. We'll need to practice it if it's to become second nature. A daily practice of looking at how we have moved in the world, how we have or have not lived according to our ethical beliefs, allows us to develop that second sense. Rather than occasional flashes of insight into ourselves or irregular contact with our spiritual selves, this ongoing practice brings us to the true steadiness and peace that come only with ongoing spiritual work. We stop dabbling in "the spiritual"—as if "the spiritual" is outside of ourselves, or "the world of the Spirit" outside of right here and now—and begin to truly *live* in a spiritual place.

Many of us have carried around the idea that "the spiritual" was indeed separate and that spiritual practice necessarily entailed all sorts of bells and whistles to make it count. Not so. An ongoing inventory of our internal lives and external actions is about as simple as it gets and is, without question, a spiritual practice. The goal is to become ethically sound, morally integrated, spiritually alive citizens of the human community; that's a spiritual goal, and one we can achieve with daily work.

An inventory can take several forms, but the purpose it serves is, essentially, to cleanse. Our major inventory in Step Four allowed us to see ourselves clearly and to make peace with ourselves and our pasts. That housecleaning was one of those monumental spiritual moments for many of us. Less momentous, on the surface, but equally important, are our daily inventories. These help prevent the pileup of emotional wreckage—some small, some large—that necessarily occurs when you happen to be a human being among other human beings. Our mistakes, our resentments, our guilt over harm done, our reaction to harm done to us—all this has a habit of collecting in our heads and taking up an enormous, messy amount of space.

Daily inventory is how we clear out the clutter, leaving us room to think with clarity again, to hear our spiritual voice, to consider what happened, and to think about how to prevent it from happening again.

What happens if we don't do these inventories? The clutter accumulates pretty fast. We start slogging around with our pet burden. Our ability to see ourselves clearly disappears; our ability and willingness to see others with any kind of generosity and open-mindedness goes out the window as well. That "daily reprieve" based on maintenance of our spiritual condition is no longer ours. A lot of people find themselves on dry drunks, emotionally mangled, spiritually gasping for air. And a lot of people find themselves on plain old *drunks*. The regular inventory, which is so easy to overlook, blow off, or set aside, is also one of the easiest ways to keep our sobriety and maintain our spiritual integrity and peace from day to day.

Step Ten is often considered the first of three "maintenance Steps," which we reach after a huge amount of spiritual work and change. These Steps, starting with Ten, focus on bringing all we've learned in the Twelve Step program so far into our daily lives. It is critical to remember that our Step work is not a to-do list. These aren't hoops we jump through in order to reach the endpoint of sobriety. Sobriety, like spirituality, is a process. These Steps, beginning with our inventories, keep us mindful of the fact that our spiritual lives are inseparable from our daily lives. Spirituality is not something we can afford to reach for only when we're in trouble; it's something we need to integrate into everything we do. These last three Steps give us a way to do that.

We have asked before, What is my moral compass, if not a God? The work we've done already has shown us that an ethics of responsibility to the human community is one that has rich spiritual rewards, one that guides us through our lives in peaceful relationship with others, always striving to offer up what we can. An active practice of self-examination, of daily inventory, keeps us ever mindful of our impact on the world. Over time, this practice also increases our willingness by leaps and bounds—willingness to change, to listen, to respect, to appreciate, to love.

The spiritual principle of responsibility is a practical manifestation of the spiritual state of love. As we love the world more deeply, fear it less, give it more, we become more deeply spiritual people—empathetic, respectful, grateful for all that we have, and willing to give all that we can. We have finally become members of the human community and are reaping the enormous rewards of living among others, no longer alone. The lesson of daily spiritual practice is not a complicated one and requires no special equipment; we are simply learning to love. That, at the end of the day, is where a spiritual practice takes us: out into the world, living in and loving this world of the spirit, here and now.

CHAPTER NINE

Spiritual Growth

November

As the cycle of the year comes to a close, and therefore nears new beginnings, we are drawn inward once again to the place where we can move more deeply into spiritual growth. For those of us who do not know a God, what can we mean by prayer? How can prayer and meditation become a part of spiritual practice for the nonbeliever? We are challenged to find ways of understanding and practicing nontheistic prayer, ways of finding through meditation a keener awareness of the spiritual voice and the need to maintain a continuous state of spiritual preparation—a practice of waiting. We have come to Step Eleven.

I sat reading in the cabin at the lake, seeking guidance in yet another book that promised me a path to God. I closed the book, set it down on the table to my left, and let the realization sink in: I simply did not believe. It was early morning, maybe four or five. I looked at the dark window, saw only my own hazy reflection, and turned off the light. I gathered up the quilts I had slung over my shoulders and went trailing across the room like a child in her mother's nightgown. I opened the door, was hit with a blast of November wind, and stepped out onto the porch.

My quilts and I curled up in the rocking chair and began to rock, the frozen wicker squeaking on the porch floor. Through the porch screen, I studied the dark. It was a deep dark, nearly black, and somehow tactile, as if you could thrust your hands into it and gather up its smooth cloth. There were no stars, only a thin scattering of gold lights curved along the opposite shore of the lake that lay invisibly out there. I knew this dark so well I could have mapped it for you, if you'd said I should—could have scribbled it on paper, telling you, *The lake pools and ripples from here to here, and the curly oak rises up here, and the fence is here, and the chair where the neighbor sits each night watching the sunset, where he has always sat and maybe always will, is here, and here is his sleeping dog, and over here, in the water, is the sandbar you have to watch out for, you'll run aground if you don't, and here is the cove where I learned to fish and wore my father's fishing hat, which kept falling into my face, I still have the hat* . . . I could have mapped that dark. I could have told you that today the light would begin to rise around seven—hours from now—and that one by one, these things would emerge from the dark, first the oak, then the neighbor's chair, the dog, the fence, and at last the lake, sketching themselves in black pen against the changing sky. And I could've told you that in a few days, we curious humans would impose our will on time itself, turn our clocks backward, try to catch that extra hour of light in the morning, before day begins.

Sitting out there on the porch, I laughed. How funny—to think of us turning our clocks this way and that, importantly telling the sun when to rise and when to set, when we would prefer it to be light and when dark. For that matter, how funny to think of us trying to impose an order on time at all. I have always loved the fact that time is a construct, invented for our convenience and probably our comfort. We take comfort in order; we are anxious little creatures and like for things to be meted out in minutes, exactly so many minutes for everything, when in fact time goes sprawling in every direction in space, bends and bounces back, takes light-years to reach one destination and reaches another at the speed of light. So in a few days, the light would slowly seep upward through the sky in exactly the fashion it did that day, and we would tinker with our clocks and say we made the planet spin at a different rate.

November morning, wickedly cold. I wrapped the quilts tighter around me, crossed my feet in their thick socks. I kept studying the dark, wishing somehow to go swimming in it, to dive headfirst off Earth and out into the first tier of space, swimming through stars and the brightly colored planets

I remember from childhood books, to go skating on Jupiter's rings—and then to sail through whatever force holds this galaxy inward, keeps it from scattering, keeps us held by our feet to the ground as we spin. I wanted to sail through whatever that force is called and into the next room of space, and then the next, and the next, so that I could get the true *feel* of infinity, finally be able to conceive of the infinite, the endless, finally be able to explain to myself what *no boundary, no end* really means.

But I'm a finite little being, here in my quilts and wool socks. I mess with clocks. I am stuck to my rocking chair, stuck to my porch, stuck to the ground. I could walk all the way around the world and not fall off. Some force—gravity, of course, that one I know—keeps me hinged to the planet, hinged to my shadow, keeps me from flying off all willy-nilly into space.

Which, it strikes me, is astonishing. Maybe even miraculous. And so is the bending and snapping back of time. And so are Jupiter's rings of smoke and stars, and so are the galaxies beyond galaxies beyond galaxies, and so is the fact of the infinite, even if I cannot grasp it in my time-bound mind.

I stop rocking. I sit in silence. I sit feeling tiny. Infinitesimal, a speck of a thing, a mote of light.

It is the feeling of wonder. Of awe.

This is not the part of the story where I say I felt the presence of God. There was no sudden thought of *Who made all this? Where did this come from?* There was no question of origins or ends. There was wonder, there was awe, in the face of all I do not know, all I cannot understand, all that is *truly* infinite, has neither origin nor end. Has no name, no face. Has no hand that will reach down and touch my own.

And I felt peace seeping through me, just as the barest beginnings of light began to seep up the sky.

The book I'd set down in the house was not a bad book. It just happened to be the one that brought to my attention the fact that I did not believe. Maybe had never believed. I had tried, off and on for my entire life, to believe. That November morning, I'd been on a mission to believe. My Twelve Step companions had told me again and again that I risked relapse if I didn't believe—in something. A God of your understanding, they said. A doorknob, the group. Whatever. But the implication, always, was that soon enough, I'd come around. I'd believe in a God. A deity, a Someone Up There.

So I waited. I tried. I acted as if. I worked the Steps. I worked with people. Every morning, I read my meditations, said some prayers I'd been told I should say.

And still I did not believe in anything resembling a God. It worried me terribly. I was certain I'd get drunk. Magically, as if *made* to get drunk by the God in whom I did not believe, as if to say, *See? Told you so.* People told me their stories—of believing in God, of believing in the Divine, of believing in The Power of Love, of believing in The Intelligent Creator. Something That Made All This. Some origin, some end.

I told them I believed in math. Chaos, I said. Infinity. That sort of thing.

They looked at me in despair.

November morning. The sky turning from indigo to violet blue, the curly oak sketched in black on the sky. Steam rising off the lake. I sat in absolute stillness, absolute peace.

This, too, is prayer.

Time curved around the planet. Prisms of light bounced and bent. Stars exploded and died a thousand years from now. Inside their houses, people fiddled with clocks.

And then, suddenly, a floating flock of loons stood up in the water—they do that, it's how they take off—beat their black and white wings wildly, and rose up out of the purple mist that hovered on the surface of the lake. They flew into the air, drew themselves into formation—who decides who flies first?—and flew south.

—

People have asked me before: What brings you comfort, if not God? To whom do you address your prayers?

And I've said, Why do I have to pray to a *whom*? Why do I have to pray *to* a thing, a being, a God? Can't I just pray?

I have had very little success explaining the way I pray to believers. To a believer—and this is perfectly acceptable, it works for them—prayer implies an object to whom (or at which) one directs one's supplications and praise. It implies a conversation of sorts; I speak, God listens, and, if I'm lucky, replies. But at least there's a God there, off whom to bounce thoughts, with whom to converse, to whom one can send up a signal when one is in trouble, whether spiritually or otherwise.

I like this idea. I agree that it's comforting. I think it would indeed bring me comfort, if I felt it deep within, if I felt the kind of awe at a God that believers seem to feel. And I do feel awe—often, profoundly, a wordless awe that takes my breath away. My awe, though, does not find its focus in a God.

And I am well aware that there are spiritual wounds that want healing. Spiritual aches that want soothing. A spiritual self that *does* want comfort, craves it deeply, in fact requires it. Something must comfort us. That something, for many people, is one kind of prayer—their conscious contact with a God.

So believers and I part ways, in fact, on only this point: I do not feel that the comfort of conversing with a God is the only kind of spiritual comfort one can find. I feel that one can be deeply comforted by spiritual sources other than a God. I do believe that our spiritual wounds can be healed here, by one another, by our own spiritual practice, and by the power of our ongoing spiritual growth.

I do not claim that we are healed by math (much as it causes me awe). It may come as a surprise, I suppose, but I believe that one way we are comforted—one way we are spiritually sustained—is through prayer. But the essence of prayer, the prayer that I practice and understand, is not that it is directed to a deity. It is, rather, an ongoing state of awareness. Awareness of others and of one's spiritual self, needs, wounds, and goals. Prayer, as a practice, is the ongoing development of a deep and constant awareness of one's spiritual life in this world.

This continuous awareness that one *is* spiritual, *has* spirit, is one spirit among millions of spiritual people, is comforting, healing, and sustaining to me. True, it is not the comfort of a God the Father or Mother or Person of any kind. It is the comfort of being held by the community of all living things, being an integral part of that community—as each of us is—and offering something to it. Meditation and prayer are where I reach deep enough to know what I have to offer and what I need. The practice of meditation and prayer deepen, daily, my ability to serve, to give, and to receive.

As we begin our consideration of what prayer and meditation can be to the nonbeliever, what form they can take, what function they serve, I want to ask this question: As spiritual beings, what do we crave? If we did know a God, what would we ask? What would we say? How would we express pain, or fear, or wonder, or thanks? What cosmic questions do we have that we would want a God to answer? What spiritual wholeness do we long for that prayer might bring?

These are things I, and many nonbelievers, take up in prayer and meditation every day. We ask cosmic questions. We speak of pain and give thanks. We argue a point, or several points. We ask for things we may or may not need, and perhaps should or should not have. But, above all, we practice. Prayer, in this sense, can be understood simply as the practice of spiritual awareness—of our questions, our wounds and wisdom, our engagement with others, and our connection to this spiritual world. And it is in prayer and meditation that we receive the answers we need—not all at once, not always with ease. But answers, comfort, and healing do come, if we remain open to their arrival.

We have only to wait.

But we have to *actively* wait. Prayer and meditation are an integral part of that active practice of waiting and of developing an ongoing, constant spiritual consciousness.

Many of us are unfamiliar with—or alienated from—an internal spiritual practice such as prayer. I have tried to show that the Twelve Steps can be much more approachable to a nonbeliever than we may have originally thought; most of them require practical action, and developing a spiritual practice based on results-oriented action turns out to be very doable. But in some ways, we have not yet been challenged on a particularly touchy front: while we have had to take spiritually based action, we have not had to figure out a practice of spiritual *consciousness*. And it doesn't come automatically. Just because we're more in touch with our spiritual selves than we have been in the past, just because we're connecting with others on a spiritual level and living with some spiritual principles in mind, doesn't mean we're done developing our spiritual lives. Hence the wording of Step Eleven: "Sought through prayer and meditation to improve our conscious contact with God *as we understood Him.* . . ." Set aside the words *with God* and *Him.* Our goal here is to continue *to improve our conscious awareness* of our spiritual nature and spiritual lives.

And if we are to do that, we need an internal practice to support our work in the world. We will not be spiritually functional without such a practice; our attempts at action will have no foundation and will be empty of meaning. But the very word *prayer* sends many of us running for the door; it leaves others simply scratching our heads, saying, To whom?

Our confusion about, and in some cases rejection of, prayer, isn't aided much by the older Twelve Step literature. The material on Step Eleven leaves less room for interpretation of spiritual source than the literature on any other Step. So we have to do some picking through the language to get to the heart of the message, which really is this: *pray.* To get to that, though, we have to get past *Twelve Steps and Twelve Traditions'* patronizing description of nonbelievers as "those one-time agnostics who still cling to the A.A. group as their higher power" (page 96). It's one of the more blatant examples of the unfortunate message that the Twelve Step programs sometimes send, which is that you are allowed to believe in whatever Higher Power you want ("God *as we understood Him*") for now—but eventually you'll come around and believe in the same Higher Power as everyone else ("God as *I* understand Him"). There sometimes seems to be very little room for an individual's spirituality, and that can make a person highly suspicious of meditation and prayer—it can feel as if those are religious, rather than spiritual, practices.

But truly they're spiritual and can take any form that works for you ("meditation and prayer *as you understand them*"). And *Twelve Steps and Twelve Traditions,* regrettable tone aside, makes an excellent point, saying that many of us "recoiled from meditation and prayer as obstinately as the scientist who refused to perform a certain experiment lest it prove his pet theory wrong" (page 97). True enough—many nonbelievers hold a real disdain for prayer and meditation, dismissing it as the opiate of the masses, etc., and never recognizing any purpose it might serve in their own non-believing lives. The implication in *Twelve Steps and Twelve Traditions* is, of course, that nonbelievers secretly fear prayer will make converts of them. I think this is probably not the case; I think most of us just don't bother because we think we have no use for prayer or, at best, have no one to pray *to*.

I believe that we do have a use for meditation and prayer, though, and our worry about who we're praying to is really very silly. We're talking to whomever and whatever we want, including ourselves. *The point is the practice of becoming spiritually aware.* By putting our spiritual lives into words—by giving language and voice to spiritual longing, pain, rejoicing, ennui—we increase our constant spiritual awareness. By developing an on-going practice of bringing our spiritual lives into consciousness, we develop greater spiritual strength and the capacity to comfort and heal one another and ourselves.

And that is the purpose of meditation and prayer: to be of use in our own and others' lives and to bring comfort to a beleaguered world. Just as our goal in Step Ten was to "grow in effectiveness" in our relationships and our daily lives, the goal of Step Eleven is to grow in *usefulness* to those around us by being aware of our spiritual needs so that we can recognize them in others as well.

Twelve Steps and Twelve Traditions makes another good point about the purpose—and utilitarian nature—of prayer: without it, it says, we "deprive our minds, our emotions, and our intuitions of vitally needed support. As the body can fail its purpose for lack of nourishment, so can the soul" (page 97).

Prayer and meditation are a method of making oneself ready. Not *for* anything in particular—we do not need to make ourselves spiritually ready *for* something any more than we need to pray *to* something. Prayer, meditation, and spiritual preparation are elements of a process that doesn't end. We move toward a state of heightened consciousness and deepened awareness of our inner lives and of the world in which we live. We reach for a greater ability to remain in constant spiritual connection—not broken into mind/body/spirit but one integrated being, aware of the integrated nature of everything around us. We practice an active state of waiting, and in doing so, we ready ourselves for all seasons of the spirit.

This is what we mean by "improving conscious contact"—we are developing and strengthening our contact with the spiritual part of ourselves, the spiritual elements of the world, whatever form they may take, whenever they may occur.

The practice of prayer and meditation will take different forms for different people. We require different amounts of structure in support of our contemplative lives; some will find it useful to adapt prayers they know or learn so that they are useful to them, while others find it useful to pray more spontaneously. The practice of meditation, too, is supported by different practices; formal meditation practice works beautifully for some, while others feel it's too restrictive. It is simply a matter of exploring various prayer and meditative practices to find the ones that feed your spiritual needs.

We are, in some ways, reframing prayer for ourselves: the prayers we say are not necessarily in the form of a direct address, said to a listener of any kind; they may be simple statements of spiritual need or gratitude that we make in our own minds. This is, generally speaking, how I pray. If I am pressed to define who or what I'm addressing, I think it's possible that I'm talking to my wisest, most spiritually evolved self, the part of me I often bury under superficial concerns, ego-driven nonsense, and the general clutter of my daily life. As I pray, I am reaching for the moral and spiritual wisdom I contain, and I'm also opening myself to the wisdom and spiritual guidance that come from the world in which I live.

Prayer, in this sense, is very practical: it allows us to tap into the parts of ourselves, and the wisdom of the world, that help us live responsibly, happily, and well. And so it makes sense to begin in a practical fashion: at the outset of each day, I often run through the Twelve Steps in my mind, think of the spiritual principles behind them, and remind myself to live that day according to those spiritual guides. I pay particular attention, in my morning prayers, to Step Three: Made a decision to turn our will and our lives over to the care of God *as we understood Him.* I make a decision, each day, to let go of my will and to live in willingness instead. This is a matter of opening the spirit in readiness for whatever the day may bring.

The Big Book recommends that as we begin our day, we "ask God to direct our thinking"; for the nonbeliever, we turn to the moral and ethical foundation we have built and are continuing to build as a guide for how we should think, and act, in the day ahead. We are reminded to pray especially that our thoughts "be divorced from self-pitying, dishonest, or self-seeking motives," and this is an excellent point—those motives yank us away from the very moral compass we need to guide our decisions, pulling us out of spirit and into ego, and therefore away from others. Ultimately, what we are preparing for in prayer each morning is to be a committed, useful part of the human community in that day, in whatever way we can be.

In looking ahead at the day, I try to remember that there is only so much we know or can guess at, and very little we can control. So instead of looking forward and setting out various wishes and demands for what I want out of that day, I find it helpful simply to put myself in a mental and spiritual state of waiting—of trusting what will come and of trusting my own spiritual capacity to work with that. I have spent a lot of time "praying" for something I didn't need and should never have had, which is a waste of effort and simply exercises the muscles of my self-will, rather than the muscles of my spiritual awareness. It's essential to me now to put faith in my spiritual readiness, rather than any self-willed "power" I might imagine that I have.

As we close our morning prayer time, the Big Book recommends that we ask "that we be shown all through the day what our next step is to be, that we be given whatever we need to take care of such problems. . . . We ask especially for freedom from self-will" (page 87). This is one of those times when one can sometimes wish for faith in a God that would both tell one what to do and give one the means with which to do it, without fail. But I personally don't share that faith and find that instead, as I close my morning prayer time, I must make a commitment to remain ever mindful of others, aware of the world in which I live, conscious of all I have to be grateful for, and willing to do all that I have to do. I make a commitment to letting go of my will whenever I realize I've taken hold of it again; and I make a commitment, finally, to live according to the moral and ethical beliefs that I hold dear. Lacking a God to instruct me, I believe it is necessary to learn to rely on a very strong ethical structure within myself, a structure informed first and foremost by the needs of others—the needs of the world in which I live.

And a useful prayer to say, setting out, is a prayer for help. You aren't asking any specific person or Person—you're simply opening yourself to the assistance of the infinite forces, internal and external, that can help guide you in living a mindful, spiritual life. A friend of mine has pasted on her steering wheel a sign to keep her aware of her own limited nature and her own need to stay spiritually aware. The sign says, "Please help!"

And that's as useful a prayer as ever I've heard.

The Big Book suggests that we review our day in the evening, focusing on whether we've thought mostly of ourselves or of others, and whether we've made ourselves useful. It reminds us "not to drift into worry, remorse or morbid reflection, for that would diminish our usefulness to others" (page 86). Here again we're reminded of the purpose of prayer—it makes us more and more able to give of ourselves and live as productive members of the human community. It isn't to get us into heaven, nor is it to get us a parking spot or win us the lottery—it is simply to make our journey through this world a peaceful and useful one. So at the end of the day, we can ask if that day's portion of the journey was peaceful, was useful, or was not.

When we've made mistakes, harmed others in any way, our prayer can focus on becoming attuned to what the morally imperative next step might be. Sometimes we will need to make an amend or ask forgiveness of others; sometimes the errors we've made have caused damage to our own spiritual or mental wellness, and the forgiveness we need to ask is our own. As we wind down our day, we prepare our spirits for rest and for beginning a new day ready to make the changes that need to be made, a new day in which to do—as the very useful saying goes—"the next right thing." Looking again to the ethical and moral foundations of our spirituality, and the work we've done in earlier Steps, we often find the guidance we need within ourselves and the good sense to seek the guidance of others as well.

And perhaps the most important part of my evening prayer practice is simply this: I express gratitude. To whom? Doesn't matter—it doesn't have to be to anyone. The assumption that gratitude must be directed to someone or must be for something, is, I think, quite false; I practice gratitude as a habit. I try to maintain a constant state of thankfulness; this is something I've learned from people who've found a great deal of serenity in their lives. There's a religious concept here that is useful: the notion of *grace*, something that is given without reason, something for which we can be thankful just because it *is*. There is so much in my life, and in the world, that seems to me an expression of grace, that I feel it's only sensible I should be in constant expression of thanks. I give thanks, often enough, for the sheer good luck to be human in this difficult world, here and now, with what I have.

Once, years ago, my friend Lora was falling asleep on my couch after a hell of a hard day during a very hard time in her life. I was sitting on the floor while she fell asleep, listening to her chatter fade and scatter into nonsense. And then, in the half-dark, half-asleep, her eyes closed, she smiled and said, "I heard once that the only really necessary prayer is *Thank you.*" And she fell promptly asleep.

And maybe it's true; maybe that is the only really necessary prayer. It is certainly indispensable.

As to guidance throughout each day, the Big Book recommends that "we pause, when agitated or doubtful, and ask for the right thought or action" (page 87). Just as a believer feels guided in that moment by a God, so nonbelievers can feel the guidance of the inner wisdom that is simple spiritual awareness. In those agitated or doubtful moments, we ask ourselves, and often other people we trust, what the most spiritually responsible thought or action would be. Here, too, we wait. We no longer need to bulldoze through our lives, no longer need to know everything this very second, no longer need to act immediately. This approach, whether practiced by a believer or a nonbeliever, will have the same benefits, among them the fact that, as the Big Book points out, we will be "in much less danger of excitement, fear, anger, worry, self-pity, or foolish decisions" (page 88). Instead, this type of prayerful approach to daily choices encourages thoughtful action, born of waiting, contemplating, and listening to our spiritual voice.

When we reach a point where a decision needs to be made, as happens constantly in our daily lives, the Big Book says we should ask God for "inspiration, an intuitive thought or decision" (page 86). Those of us who do not believe in a God are no less intuitive and no less capable of inspiration, if only we remain open to it. Prayer, as we practice it, and meditation, do open us to spiritual knowledge and wisdom that we contain and find all around us. For a long time, we have been divorced from our spiritual selves and from that intuitive sense. With the practice of prayer and meditation, we reacquaint ourselves with that intuitive knowledge, and it becomes easily accessible to us. We gradually begin to trust our own ability to make spiritually based choices and become aware of a constant spiritual consciousness. We bring spiritual attention to every area of our lives and wait for guidance in all our actions, all our thoughts.

Meditation is one way in which we can practice keeping ourselves spiritually alert and vitally aware of everything within and around us. Prayer, someone said to me recently, is simply meditation with words. Not everyone makes a distinction between meditation and prayer, but if such a distinction is to be made, that one works for me. Meditation *without* words, then, is what I use to clear the endlessly regenerated clutter with which my brain tends to fill itself. It's how I turn the volume down on my internal chatter and clear space in myself for the sound of my spiritual voice. Meditation lifts the weight of worry, the weight of ego, the weight of will, and leaves the spirit light and able to more freely move.

Meditation doesn't have to be a complicated process—in fact, it probably shouldn't be. It can be as basic as simply listening. We listen first to the flow of our breath, the beat of our blood, and the sounds that surround us. We become aware of our own physicality, our human body, firmly attached to the ground. As we pay attention to our breath, we'll hear the usual chatter in our heads grow to a fever pitch as ego and self-consciousness battle for attention. And as we keep breathing, that chatter will die down. We'll hear the deeper messages we need to listen to in that moment. With each breath, we steady ourselves and open ourselves to spiritual guidance from within. We do this as long as we are able, lengthening the practice a little each day until we have a comfortable meditative practice that gives us a kind of clearing in our day—a place free from worry or even thought, a place where we can simply open up and be still.

The practices of meditation and prayer—simply the practice of constant spiritual awareness—keep us spiritually fit, ready for whatever decisions we'll encounter, able to make choices based on spiritual principles, and able to feel the balancing force of our own ethical and moral compass.

There is one prayer—or meditation in words—that I believe can be as useful to the nonbeliever as to anyone who believes in a God. It is included in its traditional form in *Twelve Steps and Twelve Traditions*, using a direct form of address to a God, but here I'll frame it simply as a prayer or meditation one can say with the simple goal of bringing oneself to greater spiritual attention and awareness. It goes to the heart of the reason we pray and meditate, the reason for spiritual awareness in all its forms, which is to be a useful, contributing participant in this world, here and now. It is the (slightly altered) Prayer of St. Francis:

> *Make me a channel of thy peace.*
> *That where there is hatred, I may bring love;*
> *that where there is wrong, I may bring the spirit of forgiveness;*
> *that where there is discord, I may bring harmony;*
> *that where there is error, I may bring truth;*
> *that where there is doubt, I may bring faith;*
> *that where there is despair, I may bring hope;*
> *that where there are shadows, I may bring light;*
> *that where there is sadness, I may bring joy.*
>
> *Grant that I may seek rather to comfort than to be comforted;*
> *to understand than to be understood;*
> *to love than to be loved.*
> *For it is by self-forgetting that one finds.*

There have been times in my life when I felt that unbelief was by definition a nonspiritual state. I no longer feel that is the case, and it is the practice of prayer and meditation in my life that has changed my mind. While I understand the spiritual longing one feels, at times, for a comforting external force such as a God, I find that longing is assuaged by the peace of mind that contemplative practices bring. In meditation and prayer, those methods of "conscious contact" with the deepest spiritual wisdom available to us, we develop a habit of peacefulness and acceptance that bring a profound level of comfort as well. There is spiritual quietude in the acceptance of unknowing. There is great joy in loving the world and its occupants as they are, in loving one's life as it is. There are spiritual riches in being ever-present, ever-aware to the simple grace—perhaps the sheer *luck*—of being human, with so many flaws and so much to give.

CHAPTER TEN

Spiritual Action in the World

December

The religious tradition of Advent, a season of waiting, is useful as this year in the life of finding a spiritual self comes to a close. We sense the transformation we have felt in this spiritual life cycle is only a beginning, not an end in itself; transformation takes place slowly, in seasons, and will take place again, transforming us differently every time. As we continue to open our hands and let go of all we've held too hard, we find ourselves not empty, not lacking, as we'd once feared, but filled with gifts we can offer the world. This is where we learn the practice of spiritual action in the world, giving away when we most want to cling, offering up what has been offered to us, reaching beyond the desire to meet our own hungers and needs to meet the greater needs and hungers of the world. A spiritual experience, we often find, does not take place in isolation, between one self and one God; it often takes place as a connection here and now, between spiritual people, between self and world. In the practice of spiritual action, we find true healing, true growth, and spiritual experiences beyond what we can know alone. We have come to Step Twelve.

The streets seemed abandoned in that part of town. Houses leaned to one side or slowly collapsed into their centers, some of them tiny, some of them massive, a long-ago grandeur almost visible in their arched broken windows and broad sagging porches. A few houses were boarded up; others were perfectly tidy, red-checked curtains in the kitchen windows, the paint on the siding precise and white and new. But no one was visible in those windows, and no one walked along the sidewalks piled with the mountains of soot-blackened snow.

A warm day last week had melted some of the snow, and then a cold snap had caught the water where it ran down the sides of the street. Now, in the gutters, there was a clutter of cans and bottles, a headless pink doll, a frostbitten blue tennis shoe, immobilized in ice. I drove slowly through the streets at the edge of the city, looking at the holiday decorations, strings of lights, plastic Santas and snowmen and reindeer, neon crosses, enormous nativity scenes set up in the yards.

I was on my way to church.

I was a few months sober. Those months had been spent in a strange limbo; I drifted through my days, uncertain of what my life was, who I was, how I was supposed to live. I knew no better than to live according to the dictates and order of my addiction, but I had let that go, and now I did not know what to do. But I wanted to *do* something—not just go through the daily-ness of work and sleep, but something more, maybe something useful, something out in the world I'd been shut away from for so long. I felt both wildly, piercingly glad to be alive and also like I did not know what to do with the life I now held in my hands. It was as if someone had handed me the moon, and what does one do with the moon? What does one do with a life when one had expected to be dead?

But I wasn't dead. Not in body, and not in spirit anymore, either. The state of spiritual death I'd known so long had faded and been replaced with a tentative, raw, new spiritual life. But I knew that I was still only steps away from the person I'd been in my addiction. I knew that further spiritual growth was necessary if I wanted to hang on to this life. And I wanted to be more than I was.

So I was on my way to a crumbling church at the far edge of town on a brutally cold December day. This church housed a homeless shelter. They'd advertised for someone to come read to the children who stayed there. I had no earthly idea what had gotten into me. I knew nothing about children. They made me nervous. They were noisy and busy and full of questions and vividly, shriekingly alive.

The very idea of them terrified me. I still felt frozen—not the freeze of winter that goes deep below the surface, but a still-present crust of ice that covered me from head to foot, holding in what felt like this fragile self, almost newborn, and unknown to me. It seemed to me that children could be a dangerous thing when one was feeling fragile, when one's ice crust was close to cracking, and when what lay beneath was so vulnerable and raw. It seemed they might be prone to smash right into a person and send ice scattering every which way.

And they did.

I walked down the back stairs of the church—how churches all smell like *church*, I don't know—the roar of people rising as I went. I stepped into an enormous basement room, crowded with bodies, faces laughing, faces yelling, faces still and expressionless in a way that sent a chill through me. Neatly made makeshift beds lined the walls, small bundles of possessions tucked under pillows or under coats that passed for pillows. The walls were covered with drawings by the children who spent their nights on this hard floor. Every last drawing was a drawing of a house. Some also had a tree, a yellow sun, a fence, crayon flowers in the yard. But they all had a house.

I stood there looking for a person who might know what I was supposed to do.

"WHO ARE YOU?" I looked down just in time to see a tiny force in a red jacket careening toward me. The force, not quite four feet tall, crashed into my knees, flung her arms around my legs, stared up at me, and hollered, "WHATCHA DOIN' HERE?"

The force had carried on her tailwind a whole herd of children, children of various degrees of smallness, children running toward me, children sidling toward me suspiciously, or sidling shyly, hands twisted behind their backs, glancing at me sidelong to see what I'd do next.

I did not know what to do next.

I was then caught up in an amoeba-like, moving, seething crush of tiny beings whose collective force, velocity, and volume was something quite astonishing. Unable to answer all questions as to my presence and purpose at once, I finally shouted, "I'm the reading lady!"

There was a sudden pause. Then they roared and shrieked and propelled me to the sole couch in the basement, which they had turned into a fort, and as we went, their questions tumbled over each other like puppies: Where are the books? What books did you bring? Will you let me read? I have a book, read my book! Can we write a book? What grade are you in? Are you a teacher, or just a Reading Lady? Do you have a house? Where is your house? How long have you lived in a house? Do you have books in your house?

Yes, I whispered, crawling into the fort with them. They climbed over me as if I were a jungle gym. They jostled for part of a lap. They didn't notice the tears leaking out of my eyes. *Yes,* I said. *I have a house. I have books in my house.*

We read every book I'd brought. We read every book they had tucked in their tiny parcels of worldly goods. They fell asleep on me; they leaned against me with the impossible weight of small bodies; they sucked their thumbs and idly played with my hair while I read.

We sat in our complicated house of couch cushions, for those few hours our home. In that church basement, on the crumbling north side of town, we hunkered down and held our ground on this small patch of spinning world.

And so my spiritual awakening began when someone asked something of me, and I gave it to them because I had it.

Simple: They needed. I gave.

But they gave me more.

When parents called the children for dinner, we crawled out of the fort. I carried one small boy, three or four, who was so heavily asleep in my lap that he'd missed the whole thing. He woke up slightly, looked at me in confusion, decided I was all right, and settled his head into the crook of my neck.

"I have to go," I whispered.

"No," he said peacefully.

"Yes I do," I said.

"You won't come back."

"But I will."

"Take me to your house," he said.

"I'll be back tomorrow," I said.

He smiled, climbed out of my arms, and crossed the room to his mother, who led him to the dinner line.

I drove home through the neighborhood, alive and sparkling with Christmas lights, reflecting rainbows and prisms on the broad lawns of snow.

—

Advent. The season of waiting, of hope, and of prayer. Some wait and pray for God. But I simply wait, hope, and pray.

The winter sky at dawn, in the north, is a hazy deep red. The bare branches of the oak outside my window imprint themselves on this red sky, an intricate carving of negative space, deep black. Below, the snow-covered lawns are still, cast in the color of pale roses as the sun waits to rise. I look out the window, edged with a complicated lace of glittering ice crystals. I watch my breath appear and disappear on the glass. I breathe, watching the physical proof that I am alive, merely human, an animal body held tight by infinite forces, here at this given point in space.

Since I was a child, I've loved Advent. The deep quiet of the season, the sense of anticipation, of something to come. I loved walking to school in the morning, bundled against the cold, crunching through the rose-colored snow, under the red prairie sky. I sang as I walked, a song that began, *Oh come, oh come* . . . and I believed that something, always, would come. I had faith.

I still do. I believe, still, that something is to come. I do not believe it is a savior, a God; that is not what I hope for, pray for, or in which I have faith. I have faith in so much that defies language, the ineffable, the unknowable and unknown. I have faith that I will not know it, and cannot, and do not need to. I find a breathtaking wonder in that—in the fact that we cannot know what is, that we live in unknowing, and that we can and must trust the unknown. I am awed by all that's beyond us, which is to say, all that *is*. I find beauty in the humble nature of our limited minds, the fact that we can conceive of an infinite number of questions and answer only a few. I find comfort in my belief that our purpose, as humans, is not to know but to love, and I find our capacity for love dizzying in its infinite breadth and depth.

I have faith. Not in a God, not in the comfort of knowledge I cannot have. Not in an answer to questions of where we come from or where we'll go next. Not in a promise of certainty of any kind. I have faith in the human capacity for love, for kindness, for healing, for wisdom, for giving all that we have. I have faith in the humble human animal; I have faith in what we can be.

We cannot be God. We do not need to be. We can be human, unknowing. We can live in this unknowing as a state of spiritual grace. A state of waiting, of hope, of faith in what will be.

Advent, the season of waiting, is a useful image as this year in the life of a spiritual self comes to a close. We are moving into stillness again, this time to examine how we want to take action in the world. As we pause to take stock of where we have been, where we are now, and where we want to go next, we can see the arc of this journey more clearly. Where did we set out? What was our understanding of a spiritual life at that time; what is it now? What is it in us that we call our spirit? What keeps it alive, what feeds it, how do we nourish our spiritual selves? And, now that we are beginning to have some sense of ourselves as spiritual people, what does that say about how we should live?

For many of us, this has been a journey from isolation to community, from a sense that there was nothing in this universe to a sense that there is everything in this world. This has been a journey deeper into the spiritual self, for the purpose of reaching out beyond the self into the community of which we are finally a part.

What is a spiritual experience? Have we had one? Have we had what the Twelfth Step refers to as a "spiritual awakening"? The language is dramatic and seems to suggest a thunderbolt of some kind, a white-light moment in which we feel our spirits come to life. Some of us have felt this, certainly; but most of us have much quieter spiritual experiences, much quieter ways of awakening to the spiritual in ourselves and in our lives. What I would call my spiritual awakening is a process that continues, and I believe I have spiritual experiences all the time. My job is to stay closely attuned to the needs of my spirit and the spiritual needs of those around me; those needs, mine and theirs, intersect, and the connection we make at a spiritual level is both simple and profound. And the simplest, most profound connection I know is this: I give what I have to someone in need. This is spiritual action in the world. And it is a spiritual experience unlike any other.

Throughout the journey we've taken, we have been reminded, again and again, that the primary function of each stage was to grow in usefulness. As we reach this moment of assessment, it may become clear that the entire purpose of spiritual growth is to become more useful to those around us and to the larger world. The wonderful paradox is that as we become more useful, we also experience spiritual growth. That has been the case this entire time. We have faced doubt and despair, and in facing them have gathered the strength to face them when they come to us again and to face them with others when they need our support. We have learned to let go, and in letting go of what we held, we have opened our hands to those in need. We have practiced willingness and radical acceptance, an acceptance ultimately of our own humanity; that acceptance of ourselves and our nature allows us to see the beauty in the humanness of others. We have faced our demons in a process of deep self-examination and, in facing them, have rid ourselves of our own limiting fears. We have taken our first tentative steps into the world by speaking aloud the truth of who we are and where we have been. We have felt the joy of true humility in recognizing the need for change and ongoing growth, and we have finally begun to live by the ethical standards we hold. We have begun to heal the damage we have done in our lives and in that healing process have found both spiritual connection and spiritual release. We are developing regular spiritual practices that keep us mindful of the fact that we are only one human among many, and we must care for others as well as ourselves. And we are learning ways of bringing the spiritual into the everyday, through some form of mindfulness that allows us to hear our spiritual voice and guides us in living our lives in a way that is spiritually sound.

These principles that seemed so ethereal and in many cases impossible are now a solid foundation for a real spiritual practice and a vital spiritual life. So I ask again: What is a spiritual experience? What is a spiritual awakening? *Twelve Steps and Twelve Traditions* says there are as many kinds of spiritual experiences as there are people who have them; their commonality lies in the fact that the person "has now become able to do, feel, and believe that which he could not do before on his unaided strength and resources alone" (pages 106–107).

Many people interpret this as a signal that a God is the new source of that strength. And who knows? Perhaps that's the case. But for the non-believer, it is worth considering what each of us thinks this new source of strength may be. I know that there is much I am able to do, feel, and believe that I could not before. And I believe that the source of this strength is here, in this world, in the human community of which I am a part. I believe the strength is a gift to me from those who surround me. I believe it is the result of striving—failing often, but continuing to strive—to live a responsible and ethical life. And I believe absolutely that the greatest portion of my ability to do, feel, and believe what I could not alone comes from offering what I have to another person. From giving what I have, all I have, back to the world that has given it to me.

To do that, I have to continue to grow in spiritual awareness and commitment to living a spiritual life. The fact that I am no longer trapped in addiction itself, or in the mental and emotional habits of addiction, means that I am no longer a static being and am able to grow into the person I want to become. I want what's often called "emotional sobriety." Emotional sobriety is a result of practicing spiritual principles in all my affairs, as the Twelfth Step suggests. The more I bring the spiritual into the everyday, the more I find myself possessed of peace of mind, emotional balance, and mental clarity. I had none of those things when I was still living in my addiction, and I had none of them until I began to build a spiritual foundation for my life. Hardly the far-off, abstract realm I'd always seen it as, spirituality turns out to be a practical matter of becoming a sound human being, one of open heart and mind, one of responsible living, one of spiritual action in the world.

Twelve Steps and Twelve Traditions talks about emotional sobriety as the ability to "love the whole pattern of living" (page 111). Emotional sobriety depends upon the continued practice of spiritual principles we have encountered so far—honesty, willingness, acceptance, and humility among them. We are only beginning to acquaint ourselves with these things, but as we put them into action in our lives, our lives and our relationships blossom into something entirely new. We find ourselves able to accept what comes to us, *whatever* comes to us, with a degree of courage we have never felt before. We are able to find serenity even in difficult times. In seeking out the spiritual lesson of every situation, we find ourselves staying closely attuned to our spiritual selves, when before we would have lost sight of that altogether. By staying vitally aware of what is spiritual in ourselves, in others, and in everything we face, every day, we build spiritual strength that serves us in times of need and, more important, can serve others in their need as well.

We are increasingly able to face life on life's terms—the good, the bad, the boring, and everything in between—as we were never able to do before. *Twelve Steps and Twelve Traditions* rightly points out that all conditions can be transformed into "assets, sources of growth and comfort to ourselves and those about us" (page 113). All that we encounter can become a source of spiritual learning, if we step into it with willingness and openness to what it has to teach. All *whom* we encounter, too, can be a source of spiritual connection and mutual nourishment. We have lived so long without trust or faith in others, have failed to see their spiritual nature as well as our own, that we have forgotten how to respect and how to love. Now, seeking a spiritual connection with every person we meet, we begin to see the beauty, goodness, and humanity of those who walk with us in this world.

And we do not walk here alone. In that much we can have faith. Nonbelievers often ask themselves the question, *Are we alone in the universe?* which always makes me smile. Look around. This is a very crowded planet. For years, I suffered under the delusion that I was alone, ultimately and absolutely alone; I'm not quite sure how I could possibly have thought so, given the number of lives that swirled and eddied around mine in this human stream. I thought that if I did believe in a God, if I could believe in a God, I would no longer feel that loneliness, that isolation, what some believers call "a God-sized hole" in myself. But the isolation and loneliness I felt have been replaced by a sense of enormous fullness—the fullness of life as it is, where it is, here and now. The answer I wanted, which I expected to come in the form of a God, turned out to be a much simpler answer, and much closer at hand. The answer to the question, *Am I alone?* came when I began to look not down at myself or up at the sky, but out into the world.

When we believe ourselves to be alone, we have no responsibility to this world and are answerable to no one. Having begun a spiritual journey, though, it is ever more evident to me that my responsibility to the world is great, and I am answerable to all. I have to keep this in mind constantly; I am, like many people, deeply selfish in many respects, and left to my own devices—left, really, to the devices of my ego—I will go back to my muttering, self-important, self-serving ways, forgetting that I have work to do that has nothing to do with serving myself. The only work I have to do that has *anything* to do with myself, in fact, is spiritual work. That work serves the purpose of keeping me at peace, yes, but the ultimate function of even my own peace of mind is for me to become more serviceable to the world.

And so I cannot get complacent in my own spiritual life, or my work in the world slows to a trickle and then dries up. When that happens, my spirit dries up as well. The paradox of a spiritual life is that we feed our own spirits by feeding the spirits of those we encounter, those we love, those we do not even know. This is one of the most radical perspectives that the Twelve Step program offers—that this is a "selfish" program in that we must help others out of their addiction in order to stay out of our own. Our spirits, and our lives, demand less that we receive than that we give. We must offer something. What do we offer? Anything at all. The notion that we have nothing to give is nonsense. We do not need wealth or brilliance or particular gifts of any kind. We need only our best selves, and we need to bring those out into the world in whatever way we can.

This requires effort. Telling ourselves we haven't got time to be of service won't do. We have time to be of use in this life. Perhaps that is the very function of this life; I happen to think so, but I'm no authority on why we exist and what we're for. That is for us to decide; that is our ethical responsibility, to find our own purpose in life and to follow it. Rarely have I met a happy person, a peaceful person, who believed his purpose in life was to serve himself. But most of us act as if that's the case. That's a human habit, and one that can only be broken by consistent spiritual work. The best spiritual practice I know to break us of the habit of self-serving is the service of others.

To whom should we be of service? Anyone. The world's need is very great. How? In any way that we can. Our capacity to love, to serve, is the one infinite thing that we contain. We can seek out new ways of making spiritual connections, find new forms of spiritual work, by involving ourselves with those in need, whatever their need may be. As we explore and expand our practices of service, our spiritual lives are strengthened and enriched. We tap into that infinite capacity within ourselves, deepening our own spiritual experience of the world we are in, and becoming a source of spiritual comfort and strength to someone else.

We can be a source of spiritual comfort and strength. Believers sometimes ask me, What comforts you? What gives you strength in time of trouble? Who do you turn to in need? And I say that what comforts me is comforting someone else when I can; what gives me strength is giving strength to another; and when I need, I try to give. I return to the Prayer of St. Francis: ". . . Grant that I may seek rather to comfort than to be comforted; to understand than to be understood; to love than to be loved. For it is by self-forgetting that one finds."

EPILOGUE

As this year of a spiritual search draws to a close, I can offer no neat summing up. I have as many questions as I did when I set out; that is the unfolding nature of spiritual growth. I know very little, and wonder much. I do not know where the greater journey of the world began, nor do I know where it goes. I have no universal compass, no cosmic map. I have only the sound of my own spiritual voice and the loud, unruly, beautiful song of the world I need to serve.

And so I listen. And so I sing.

1. We admitted we were powerless over alcohol—that our lives had become unmanageable.
2. Came to believe that a Power greater than ourselves could restore us to sanity.
3. Made a decision to turn our will and our lives over to the care of God *as we understood Him.*
4. Made a searching and fearless moral inventory of ourselves.
5. Admitted to God, to ourselves, and to another human being the exact nature of our wrongs.
6. Were entirely ready to have God remove all these defects of character.
7. Humbly asked Him to remove our shortcomings.
8. Made a list of all persons we had harmed, and became willing to make amends to them all.
9. Made direct amends to such people wherever possible, except when to do so would injure them or others.
10. Continued to take personal inventory and when we were wrong promptly admitted it.
11. Sought through prayer and meditation to improve our conscious contact with God *as we understood Him,* praying only for knowledge of His will for us and the power to carry that out.
12. Having had a spiritual awakening as the result of these steps, we tried to carry this message to alcoholics, and to practice these principles in all our affairs.

The Twelve Steps of AA are reprinted from *Alcoholics Anonymous,* 4th edition, published by AA World Services, Inc., 2001, New York, NY, 59–60.

ABOUT THE AUTHOR

Marya Hornbacher is an award-winning journalist and the Pulitzer Prize–nominated author of four books. Her best-selling memoirs *Madness: A Bipolar Life* and *Wasted: A Memoir of Anorexia and Bulimia* have become classics in their fields, her recovery handbook *Sane: Mental Illness, Addiction, and the 12 Steps* is an honest and enlightening look at the Twelve Steps for people who have co-occurring addiction and mental health disorders, and her critically acclaimed novel *The Center of Winter* is taught in universities all over the world. Hornbacher's work has been published in sixteen languages. She lectures regularly on writing, addiction, recovery, and mental health.